# The Recurrent Crisis in Corporate Governance

# The Recurrent Crisis in Corporate Governance

Paul W. MacAvoy

and

Ira M. Millstein

First published 2003 by
PALGRAVE MACMILLAN
Houndmills, Basingstoke, Hampshire RG21 6XS and
175 Fifth Avenue, New York, N.Y. 10010
Companies and representatives throughout the world

PALGRAVE MACMILLAN is the global academic imprint of the Palgrave Macmillan division of St. Martin's Press, LLC and of Palgrave Macmillan Ltd. Macmillan® is a registered trademark in the United States, United Kingdom and other countries. Palgrave is a registered trademark in the European Union and other countries.

ISBN 1–4039–1666–7

This book is printed on paper suitable for recycling and made from fully managed and sustained forest sources.

A catalogue record for this book is available from the British Library.

Library of Congress Cataloging-in-Publication Data
MacAvoy, Paul W.
    The recurrent crisis in corporate governance / Paul W. MacAvoy,
    Ira M. Millstein
        p.   cm.
    Includes bibliographical references and index.
    ISBN 1–4039–1666–7
    1. Corporate governance.   I. Millstein, Ira M.   II. Title.
    HD2741.M196 2003
    658.4—dc21                                                       2003048290

10   9   8   7   6   5   4   3   2
12   11   10   09   08   07   06   05   04

Printed and bound in Great Britain by
Antony Rowe Ltd, Chippenham and Eastbourne

# Contents

# List of Figures and Tables

## Figures

## Tables

# List of Appendix Tables

# Preface

For a lawyer and an economist to work together, on the same contentious problem, for more than a decade, testifies to a number of facets of a unique production process. We are good friends to such an extent that this collaboration has survived even when frequent disagreements broke out concerning the relative merits of our respective disciplines. We have continued because first one and then the other stated that the problem was not only not solved, but was worse than before. And we at last are prepared to go to print because we both believe that law together with managerial economics are both necessary, and may be sufficient, to develop effective governance of the American corporation.

Our position is based not only on the experiences of the last decade, but also on the theory and empirics of academia, and on the cottage industry of governance consulting. We began collaboration when we opposed a primarily litigious approach to corporate governance then being considered by the American Law Institute's *Principles of Corporate Governance* (1983). We initiated teaching in a course at the Yale School of Management in 1991 based on our experiences serving on boards of directors or as counsel to boards of directors. We have taught corporate governance together for the last eight years, and in that process have invited to classes for their experiences numerous Chief Executive Officers (CEOs), directors and scholars of governance. We have exchanged ideas every week at Mory's, often with the Yale faculty in law and management involved in such matters, and therefore have lost any sense of proprietorship concerning ideas on effective corporate governance. (Nevertheless, we take personal responsibility for those ideas that are written out in the chapters that follow.)

Between us we have been exposed to the inner workings of the boards of a host of companies. Paul MacAvoy has served on 14 corporate boards, including Amax Inc., Combustion Engineering, Inc., American Cyanamid Co., Chase Manhattan Bank and the Lafarge Corporation. Ira Millstein has counselled over 50 boards, including General Motors Corp., Bethlehem Steel Corp., Olympia & York Properties Corporation, Drexel Burnham Lambert Group Inc., Federated Department Stores Inc. (Macy's), Westinghouse Electric Corp., Sunbeam Corp., Tyco International Ltd. and The Walt Disney Company. He has been involved with a host of not-for-profit boards as well, including, *pro bono*, that of the Lower

Manhattan Development Corporation created after the destruction of the World Trade Center. Between us, we have observed and participated in almost every calamitous event that can occur in a boardroom, and observed directors performing well, sleeping at the board table, and everything in between.

Our conclusions take account of cited research in law, economics, and management, but are also based on long observation of process and practice in the corporate world. We are comfortable in proffering them as the solution to important, perhaps critical, problems in corporate governance that result in significant diversion of financial return that should accrue to the investor.

This statement of beliefs may cause managements, and media devoted to the imperial position of management, to lay this book aside. So be it; but for the rest, we hope you will appraise our scholar-participant approach to problem solving in governance by reading through to the end. The book is devoted to supporting a case for the board of directors, with leadership from an independent chair, putting new controls on management, and being held accountable for the result.

If boards respond to these suggestions, there is a fair chance that performance and accountability will improve and that further, more regulatory and therefore intrusive, legislation can be avoided. We would like to see corporate governance become primarily the province of well-motivated, ethical, private-sector institutions.

While Ira Millstein has for more than 30 years lectured and written widely on corporate governance, it has been his desire that the field be subjected to more rigorous academic discipline than has been the case. It has been Paul MacAvoy's desire that the academic literature be informed by broad practical experience. Hence this partnership between Ira Millstein and Paul MacAvoy, particularly in this book. Because, however, of Ira Millstein's lack of expertise in empirics, Paul MacAvoy takes sole responsibility for the chapters which bear his name alone. Paul MacAvoy indicates that the alphabetical reversal of names – Millstein and then MacAvoy – in the other chapters is meant to indicate his deference to Ira Millstein in matters relating to the creation of ideas over the years in the workings of public policy towards corporate governance. This research has, been supported by grants from the John M. Olin Foundation to Yale University. Together, we thank Ashley Altschuler, John Bodt, David Murgio and Olga Sokolova for all they have done to further the cause.

PAUL W. MACAVOY
IRA M. MILLSTEIN

# List of Abbreviations

| | |
|---|---|
| ABA | American Bar Association |
| CalPERS | California Public Employees' Retirement System |
| CAPM | capital asset pricing model |
| CEO | chief executive officer |
| CFO | chief financial officer |
| CII | Council of Institutional Investors |
| EBIT | earnings before interest and taxes |
| EBITDA | earnings before interest, taxes, depreciation and amortization |
| EPS | earnings per share |
| EVA™ | economic value added |
| GAAP | generally accepted accounting practices |
| GM | General Motors Corporation |
| LSE | London Stock Exchange |
| NACD | National Association of Corporate Directors |
| NOPLAT | net operating profit less adjusted taxes |
| NYSE | New York Stock Exchange |
| OIC | operating invested capital |
| OWC | operating working capital |
| RIOC | return on invested capital |
| ROE | Return on Equity |
| S&P | *Standard & Poor's* |
| SEC | Securities and Exchange Commission |
| TIAA-CREF | Teachers Insurance and Annuity Association – College Retirement Equities Fund |
| TSE | Toronto Stock Exchange |
| VAR | valuation at risk |
| WACC | weighted average cost of capital |

# 1

# Introduction and Summary

*Ira M. Millstein and Paul W. MacAvoy*

With fits and starts, the current governance crisis has been 30 years in the making. The decline in performance of the over-diversified, over-staffed corporation in the 1980s was marked, and blamed on management that was essentially ungoverned. A round of firings of management followed, accompanied by the creation of independent, active boards of directors. Governance reform was thought to be evolving in the late 1990s as the American corporation forged ahead in efficiency and earnings performance with strong response in stock price appreciation. No more was the imperial Chief Executive Officer (CEO) to be criticized for ignoring the rightful returns of investors; but the scandals of Enron and others, and the bursting of the bubble in stock prices of Internet, telecom and energy company shares, has caused those of us involved with the corporate enterprise to take another look. While we thought governance had reached an enviable pinnacle of excellence, at least in form, we came to realize that it had not, in substance. Substantive governance simply had not followed structural reforms.

We are sceptical that the further structural improvements mandated in the last year by the Sarbanes–Oxley Act of 2002 and related rules from the Securities and Exchange Commission (SEC), the New York Stock Exchange (NYSE) and NASDAQ will wholly suffice to change that condition. The substance of reform lies in the actual performance of boards in properly carrying out their responsibilities to shareholders and the public. This substance requires more than proper structure and process, and more can be done. Unfortunately, that 'more' is not in place.

Now, with our own recent investigations and new experience with unexpected failures in governance, we have reached conclusions as to what is missing today in corporate governance. This is what this book is all about.

We begin with the premise that the 'corporation' was a marvellous invention designed to organize labour and capital to accommodate the Industrial Revolution, and that it has justifiably survived as the principal organizing mechanism in succeeding eras of business development.

But we have to conform to the fundamental statutory construction of the corporation, which provides that 'the business and affairs of every corporation should be managed by or under the direction of the board of directors'. By law the board was, and still is, the corporation's ultimate authority. In family-owned corporations the board also manages the operations of the company because management is made up of family members. But as corporations have become progressively larger and more complex, and are no longer family-owned, management has been delegated to professional executives under more specific and complex corporate charters and by-laws. That professional cadre, over time, succeeded in recasting the ultimate responsibility of a board as 'limited to overseeing', which became progressively more limited as management exercised control, and ultimately became 'imperial'. Both small shareholders and large shareholders, such as pension and mutual funds, stood aside as this transfer of authority occurred.

Almost two decades ago we took the position along with other analysts and critics that it was necessary to return to corporate fundamentals, for boards to assert and exercise their statutory obligations and responsibilities to the shareholders who put them in place. There were positive results. In 1997, we first attempted to measure the effect of this return to basic responsibilities on earnings, and we found these effects to be widespread and substantial. More than one-third, and perhaps as many as one-half, of the largest 300 corporations had improved their earnings performance after they reformed their governance systems. Boards had only to emerge from the passive oversight created in the era of 'managerial capitalism' for earning to increase, as management focused on cost efficiencies and on profitable market opportunities. The turnaround began taking place by the mid-1990s, with widespread response to an activated board's replacement of the CEO at General Motors (GM), the distribution by the California Public Employees Retirement System (CalPERS) of the General Motors guidelines on effective governance, and the subsequent board terminations of the CEO at Westinghouse, IBM, American Express and Eastman Kodak, among others. The die was cast for effective governance through improved board structure and process and we could move on, we thought, to other issues concerning the behaviours of corporations.

The die was cast, but the new form was not universally and instantaneously followed by changes in conduct. Such a transformation required a strong board to bring about substantial change in managerial incentives and responses. It could not result solely from changing board structure and notions of board 'independence'. We thought that reform of the procedures and structure that govern the management–board relationship would be evolutionary, and would by themselves enable substantive improvements in management performance. But the taking on of responsibilities by the board depended on director attitudes, willingness to take responsibilities, and attention to duty. Because such a shift in duties and responsibilities did not obviously improve the well-being of management, even though it would lead to gains in earnings and share prices, we were unwilling to speculate on how long a change in conduct throughout corporate America would take; but at least the route seemed clear.

Since the late 1990s it has become evident that such a transformation in process and structure, even where it has taken place, has produced limited, but not sufficient, means to enable the new governance system to perform. To be effective requires that a board of directors has the ability to assess the corporation's environment, organization, personnel and political affairs, as well as resulting financial accounting practices. This ability is essential in many challenges and opportunities requiring knowledge sufficient to test management's initiatives and resulting performance. How do men and women who may spend a few hours every month as directors of a corporation gain the level of understanding and acquire the requisite information to make collective strategic assessments on a regular, ongoing basis? We know that today most directors, even under improved processes and structures, cannot claim to have the capability to conduct meaningful assessments and testing in many circumstances. Access to information or even to management is too limited; the board is taking on responsibilities without the means to fulfil its obligations.

Thus the 'recurrent crisis' is due to the incapacity to deliver in practice on heightened expectations for governance. There is a void of capability which, if not filled, will culminate again in misleading and inadequate reported financial results and large managerial extractions of wealth from failing companies. We can expect more scandal, more failure, from more self-dealing, despite newly mandated process and structural reforms. More fundamental is the recurrence of massive destruction of investor value to the loss of the economy as a whole.

What can be done? The information void must be filled. There is no current mechanism in place to do so, for we do not believe that the singular CEO/chairman can be relied upon to provide the board with what is required to be informed on sensitive issues. We cannot expect the CEO, in his other role as chairman, to prepare the board to evaluate lapses and failures on his part, or on the part of his chosen management. Nothing short of separating the roles of board leadership and management leadership will suffice. Ideally, the board's chairman should be an independent director, thus separating the roles in form as well as substance. That chairman would ensure that focused information on key issues reaches the board. That chairman could create meaningful agendas and call for management presentations around issues, not just around current problems that need resolution. He or she could chair meetings with content rather than routine, based on position papers rather than reports. That chairman, having this 'job', could spend the time and energy, with a separate staff when necessary, which is essential to fill the information void. Then, and only then, will the governance reform structures, now a decade in place, enable substantive assessments by the board, leading to gains in performance.

We recognize the strong opposition of managements to this change; they see it as stripping the authority of chairman from existing CEOs. To avoid this, we urge board action to end the duality upon succession, which now is just every few years. Active shareholders should insist on that board action, to make it clear that the new CEO is not perceived as having been downgraded. Until the titles change, an independent director (designated as 'lead' or 'presiding') can begin to fill the void, as long as the role is properly defined. Because the 'lead' or 'presiding' director is still just another director, subject to the influence if not dominance of the singular CEO/chairman, we have no confidence in that role as more than a temporary step on the road to separation. In corporate America, titles make a difference.

Directors will have to step up to their responsibilities, once they conduct their assessments of management plans and results with the additional knowledge and information ideally provided through the efforts of an independent chairman. More time, more attention, more real independence of mind, and requisite board compensation, will be essential. Their actions should lead to better management and corporate performance.

To us these initiatives should not be totally mandated by regulation or legislation. The personality, experience, and identity of the non-executive chairman (or, temporarily, the lead director) will be a matter for each board to decide for itself, as will the precise content of the chairman's role. The details of how each director fulfils his or her new role is certainly, and primarily, a question of whether that director is personally committed to take on the task. We suggest that separating the chair and CEO positions be accomplished, at the outset, through a new listing requirement to be imposed by the NYSE and NASDAQ, requiring corporations either to adopt a non-executive chairman (describing the role), or to explain (in their proxy materials) why they have not. (A temporary explanation could be the selection of a lead or presiding director.) If the bulk of corporate boards, after two years, fails to confirm, then we suggest the adoption of a compulsory requirement.

Our suggested reforms need to be seen as critically needed self-help: help to the corporation; help to the management leadership system we wish to preserve; and help to the directors themselves.

We believe a threat of shareholder litigation in the state courts will and should be an additional motivation for directors to engage in active governance of the corporation. With the newly-developed ability to determine the status of management performance relative to goals and plans, there has to be director accountability in decisions that require management to achieve markers relative to these goals and plans. The board should 'know', and it has to 'act'. Non-action in the face of management actions against the interests of shareholders should make the board itself liable for adverse results. Mistakes in judgment will be countenanced under the Business Judgment Rule, but only so long as there is a 'good faith' effort to obtain information, a 'good faith' board assessment of the material issues, and action taken in 'good faith' to resolve these issues. While there will certainly be concerns about increased director responsibility, we are convinced that the courts will know 'good faith' when they see it. For example, the failure of the board of a bank to discharge the CEO, after banking regulators demonstrate to the board that the current CEO is causing a run on deposits, would not be 'good faith' by the board. Another example: if, after two years under our proposed comply-or-explain listing requirement for separating the roles of chairman and CEO, the board does not have a reasonable explanation for not complying, its 'good faith' might well be questioned by stockholders and tested in court.

While we will make some suggestions along the way for additional structural and procedural board improvement, we do not want to dilute our most basic points: the need for increased board information and leadership through separating the roles of chairman and CEO and for ensuring that the board of directors carries out its duties in 'good faith'.

# 2
# The Current Crisis

*Ira M. Millstein and Paul W. MacAvoy*

In the space of less than twelve months in 2001–2, more than a quarter of the largest corporations in the American economy experienced downturns in current sales revenues or prospects for future revenues that caused their common share prices to fall from the $50 range to $1 or less. The levelling of gross domestic product, termed a recession by media alarmists, played a major role in this collapse, but the failure of Internet services, information technology, and telecommunications to grow as rapidly as had been forecast played an even greater role. The most spectacular declines were in equipment companies for these industries where more than $1.5 trillion of investor share value disappeared.

There are more basic explanations, however, for the collapse of share prices. The collapse of large, high-tech company share prices was said to be the result of bad strategy, recklessly and even fraudulently implemented by management. That could not have happened without dysfunctional corporate governance. Supposedly reliable management had turned to fraud, or at least deception, to achieve very large personal gains. In some instances, fraud and deception extended to the auditors, legal counsel, and the board of directors. But it was not that board participation in wrongdoing was so widespread but rather that the board did not know but arguably could have, and with knowledge could have taken steps to prevent self dealing and subsequent collapse in shareholder value.

The media stories on the collapse of those corporations touched by scandal sooner or later made reference to the Enron Corporation. The fifth largest United States corporation, with more than $100 billion in revenues in its last year before bankruptcy, Enron collapsed in the last quarter of 2001 along with 99 per cent of its stock value. The full range of reasons for Enron's tumble have been publicized, from alleged insider dealing, fraudulent accounting and excessive financial leverage to aggressive trading positions in volatile energy markets and massive investment mistakes in large construction projects in Brazil and India. But many, including the Congress, still ask, 'Where was the board of directors, and why didn't it restrain management before it brought Enron down?'

The same questions have been asked of the boards of Global Crossing, WorldCom, Lucent, Williams, Dynegy, K-Mart and HealthSouth. The business pages assert that these corporate collapses and subsequent destruction in share prices resulted from management initiatives that were reckless, self-serving or fraudulent. At the time of this writing, however, it is becoming clear that, with so many of the largest corporations failing during a period of business cycle recovery, a more inclusive explanation based on the failure of governance may be in order. We do not with 20/20 hindsight choose to indict boards of directors although we note that many of them appear to have operated with a significant degree of passivity and/or deference to management. Rather, we are searching for the cause of this too-common passivity and deference. We (and others) believe there is a governance mechanism in the engine of the corporation that is broken and has allowed an excessive number of company collapses.[1]

The 'broken engine' argument is based on certain characteristics of the corporate form of enterprise. Since inception, corporations have been founded on state charters that specify not what is to be produced, but how responsibility for the use of investor capital is to be recognized. Investor capital, in general, under state law is to be used to maximize profit returns, and the board of directors is responsible for making sure that these profits accrue to the investor. For numerous and diverse investors the board serves as an agent that appoints and monitors management to achieve this result.

In practice it has not worked out that way. Between 1960 and 1990, this system was, in general, disoriented, with the board serving as a source of support in the pursuit of management's goals. The CEO dominated both management and the board, serving as the board chairman, and appointing the board of directors to assist. It was the CEO, not the board, who determined corporate strategy as well as how earnings were to be distributed among employees, customers, community groups, and investors.

---

1 See John Plender, *Going off the Rails: Global Capital and the Crisis of Legitimacy* (2003).

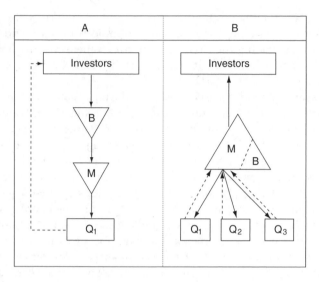

*Figure 2.1* The focus of decisions

*Note*: A and B are scenarios of corporate conduct, with B in the triangle indicating board of directors initiatives, M indicating management initiative, and Q indicating product line results.

To indicate what this shift in decision responsibility did to corporate conduct, consider Figure 2.1.

In the original pre-1960 governance system depicted by panel A, management, $M$, was given responsibility by the board, $B$, to implement plans in the interest of investors. But by 1960, board power had atrophied, resulting in management firmly in charge, with the same governance structure but a de facto configuration of practices and conduct similar to that depicted in panel B. The board was a supplementary source of ideas and support for management, who dealt with the investor as well as with buyers and competitors. The devolution of the board to a position that was advisory to management in increasingly diverse operations took place gradually as CEOs retired and new CEOs in the replacement process took the initiative. In the interests of the newly independent, expansive CEO, major acquisitions were undertaken and product lines extended to $Q_2$ and $Q_3$. To present a perception of high and stable growth, $Q_1$, $Q_2$ and $Q_3$ generated earnings that became unconnected to current cash flow, and were 'managed' by smoothing peaks and troughs by means of reserve accounts from year to year. While the result in panel A was profits to shareholders, the result in panel B was funds for expansive diversification, increased executive compensation, and, last, discretionary dividends.

The corporate governance reform movement that began in the USA in the late 1980s and early 1990s and gained attention until the latter part of the decade sought in its essentials a return to the original construct in which the board of directors was responsible. It succeeded. Significant improvements in corporate performance were realized in some large domestic corporations in which board activation was present. But this shift of control from management back to the board was not complete, and neither was it effective in improving corporate performance in the downturn phase of the economy experienced in 2000–1.

This is not to imply that there were not new sources of initiative in the board of directors of large listed US companies in general. The board, focusing on corporate results, pressured management to pay less attention to growth and more to improved earnings performance. The board always had the prerogative to change management, and generally did so when earnings deteriorated. But in the 1970s and 1980s many boards failed to take that step until the company was just short of bankruptcy. The new focus by boards on 'accountability' began to challenge management to demonstrate that it was doing its best for earnings given current limiting constraints and opportunities.

Looking back over 30 years, the 'break' in the corporate engine was that the board of directors was not functioning as agent for investors. As a result, management need not and was not using investor capital to achieve the earnings levels possible at the time. This fault began to be fixed by the late 1980s and early 1990s with the independent directors asserting control; but the collapse of numerous major corporations in the early 2000s raises the question as to whether the new director initiative achieved the required results, and, if not, then what further reforms are necessary.

In Chapter 3 we begin an inquiry into whether what was 'broke' can be fixed further by reviewing how we got where we are. This begins with how corporations were governed prior to the 1990s, how governance was transformed during that decade and what caused the change. We consider the building blocks of a strong or 'professional' board and what caused these blocks to be put in place in some corporations but not others. We consider not only how this organization of directors is structured but their conduct and responsibilities.

In Chapter 4, we examine the existing literature on board structure and process and its relationships to financial performance. We find that, at best, these are inconclusive.

In Chapter 5 we undertake our own study to determine the impact of the governance reform of the early 1990s on the performance of the large US corporations. As in our *Columbia Law Review* (June 1998) article, observation and reasonable assumptions lead us to hypothesize that corporations with a board of directors active and independent of management will monitor and incentivize management to generate higher returns for investors. As we did in our earlier article, we test this by comparing operating earnings in companies with strong governance with those of companies with passive or management-dominated governance. With numerous corporations marked by independent and active board control there should have been a difference in the performance of large corporations. Our response is affirmative.

We examine the 'recurrent' governance crisis in detail in Chapter 6, which focuses on the implications of the Enron-type problem of alleged fraudulent or misleading accounting leading to the loss of investor value in the company. Of central interest is a set of nine of the 100 largest corporations that by mid-2002 had come under investigation for securities law violations, at the same time as their earnings and share prices collapsed, and as senior executives cashed in millions of dollars of personal stock options. The question is whether reformed governance could have (and, if so, should have) prevented the collapse of these leading corporations. Our response is affirmative.

In Chapter 7 we offer proposals for further governance reform. Proposals already made by Congress, the financial regulatory institutions, and the states have been aimed at strengthening boards through enhanced listing rule requirements and the use of shareholder litigation to hold board members more directly accountable for abiding by evolving standards of corporate governance conduct. Our proposals go further, and may be viewed by some as radical, but we believe they are required for the American chartered corporation, let alone our capital market system, to survive. Our basic thrust is that there are two significant corporate roles – leading the board and managing the corporation – and that these roles require the services of two different people; that providing adequate board leadership requires a separate chairman to focus on supplying critical information to directors now lacking, and that directors should use the information to make 'good faith' decisions that require management to operate only in the interests of the corporation and its shareholders.

# 3
# The Emergence and Development of the Governance Problem

*Ira M. Millstein and Paul W. MacAvoy*

Any discussion of faults in governance has to begin with an explanation of the corporation's ultimate purpose: that is, the criteria by which the corporation's performance and success are to be measured. Throughout its development the corporation has had one stated objective: 'the conduct of business activities with a view toward enhancing corporate profit and shareholder gain'.[1] While some have argued that employees, suppliers and communities deserve at least some of the residual, or 'profit', this has generally been rejected as being in conflict with the conceptual model and state law and judicial decisions.

Corporations are not charitable organizations, and neither are they formed to undertake fund disbursal programmes determined by managers. In the abstract, the corporation is a set of contracts for inputs in production, such as land, labour and materials, all financed by owner-provided capital. While contractees have rights to income for services rendered, only owners have rights to profit after all costs have been incurred and the product has been sold. The owner bears the risk of variation in this residual profit and has then the right to disburse it or otherwise withdraw the capital. While managers should meet commitments to 'constituents' – employees, customers, suppliers and communities – these are largely contractual commitments to be discharged to enhance profitability. (The issue of the corporation's 'social responsibility' is certainly important; however, exploring any preconceived tradeoff by

---

1 American Law Institute, *Principles of Corporate Governance: Analysis and Recommendations*, 1 (1994), § 2.01(a).

management between that responsibility and agency to owners would be to negate the principal-agency relationship, that is the subject of this book. How the corporation's social responsibility is to be addressed in an evolving society is the subject of another book.)

This concept of the investor-owned 'corporation' is based on a governance system for implementation of a plan to produce goods and services of any type and variety, anywhere in the world.[2] Revenues generated from this activity pay for resources under contract except for capital which, instead of recurring contract payments, has rights to the residual of revenues in excess of other contract costs. Investors should have in place as their agent a board of directors to achieve the largest possible residual consonant with fully meeting contract requirements, legal requirements, and appropriate ethical considerations.[3]

Yet as far as actual results are concerned, it has been widely recognized that management acting in its own interests, not those of the investor or the board as the investor's agent, can and will run off course. In certain, and numerous, corporations in the 1970s and 1980s management used corporate assets contrary to shareholder interests to build over-large organizations, and/or to extend payments to asserted 'stakeholders' beyond what was required. This type of management behaviour was spelled out more than 70 years ago, in 1932, by Adolf Berle and Gardiner Means in *The Modern Corporation and Private Property*.[4] They warned that management can be expected to serve as agent for itself rather than for investors, shifting the resources of the corporation to its own agenda, whether that is to expand activities for the sake of size alone, or to protect jobs, or to increase its own compensation. Berle and Means' fear was supposed

---

2 For an entertaining description of the limited liability company as an agent of social and economic change through history, see John Micklethwait and Adrian Wooldridge, *The Company: A Short History of a Revolutionary Idea* (Random House Inc., 2003).

3 See American Law Institute, *Principals of Corporate Governance*, § 2.01; Del. Code Ann. tit. 8, § 141(a) and II.B (1974) ('The business and affairs of every corporation organized under this chapter shall be managed by or under the direction of a board of directors ... Courts will not interfere with directors' business judgment'); American Law Institute, *Principles of Corporate Governance*, § 4.01(a) (business judgment rule requires directors to perform their duties 'in the best interests of the corporation').

4 Adolf Berle and Gardiner Means, *The Modern Corporation and Private Property* (1932), 337; Adam Smith, *The Wealth of Nations* (1776). Two years later Yale Professor William O. Douglas reiterated the Berle and Means central argument: W.O. Douglas, 'Directors who do not Direct', *Harvard Law Review*, 47 (1305) (1934).

to be dispelled by making leadership in more focused organizations sweep away those who did not perform and replace them with those who would. Thus, by the 1940s and 1950s it had become apparant that the market within the corporation for control functioned imperfectly. In many cases, the process of replacing the deviant leadership swept away good management and led to mismanagement. In other cases reorganization resulted in the more efficient use of assets, but the costs of the transition were significant and the consolidation of operations was itself stretched over years before completion.

## Conglomeration as an example of managerial self-interest

More fundamentally, an acquisition process emerged by which professional outsiders gained control; that process itself went astray during the mid-1970s and the 1980s. Merger activity increased to such an extent that it became the largest 'wave' of takeovers on record. In the first part of this period, mergers were characterized by the consolidation of small to medium sized companies in unrelated industries (given that they were of roughly the same scale, the number of announcements of takeover indicates the growth and decline of this so-called 'wave'). As shown in Table 3.1, this number increased from between 2,000 and 3,000 per year to 6,000 in 1969, and stayed in the range of 4,000 to 5,000 per year until 1973. From then until 1980, it was sequentially 2,200 per year.

Media discussions of these mergers justified them by a simple theory of diversification, which held that control of a variety of businesses in a single corporation would lessen the risk of insolvency for the corporation during economy-wide downturns. The corporation in effect was a diversified portfolio of assets spread across markets affected differently

*Table 3.1* Net merger-acquisition announcements

| Year | Number | Percentage change | Year | Number | Percentage change |
|------|--------|-------------------|------|--------|-------------------|
| 1963 | 1,361 |     | 1972 | 4,801 | +4 |
| 1964 | 1,950 | 43  | 1973 | 4,040 | −16 |
| 1965 | 2,125 | +9  | 1974 | 2,861 | −29 |
| 1966 | 2,377 | 12  | 1975 | 2,297 | −20 |
| 1967 | 2,975 | 25  | 1976 | 2,276 | −1 |
| 1968 | 4,462 | 50  | 1977 | 2,224 | −2 |
| 1969 | 6,107 | 37  | 1978 | 2,106 | −5 |
| 1970 | 5,152 | −16 | 1979 | 2,128 | +1 |
| 1971 | 4,608 | −11 | 1980 | 1,889 | −11 |

by downturns or upturns in the business cycle. In addition, pooling of interest accounting was said by some to encourage these acquisitions by allowing the acquiring corporation to combine its activities (with a low price to earnings ratio) with the acquired firm's activities (with a high price to earnings per share), thereby boosting the share price of the acquiring firm. This conglomerate wave ended with the fall in share market prices during the stagflation of the economy in 1973–5; even so, very large conglomerates such as ITT, Textron, Litton and LTV emerged from this round of diversified merger activity intact.

In the 1980s the takeover phenomenon re-emerged not in large numbers of mergers, but in large sized acquisitions. The number of transactions began to decline from approximately 2,200 to 1,800 by 1980, but the dollar values of the transactions steadily increased. There were numerous 'mega deals', as designated by the media, involving hostile tender offers based on high bond leverage in the package of cash, bonds, and shares offered by the acquirer. The introduction in markets of below investment grade or 'junk bonds' made it possible for financial institutions to fund professional buyout organizations. As a result, the 1980s were the decade of highly leveraged buyouts that created more large conglomerate corporations.

That ended with the temporary disrepute of the junk bond, following the bankruptcy of Drexel Burnham, the dominant source of this method of financing. By 1990, the conglomerate corporations that were still intact were significantly larger than their non-conglomerate counterparts in terms of sales and assets. They were not larger in terms of net profits,[5] and their profits were based on higher levels of financial leverage.

Jae H. Song investigated 54 conglomerate acquisitions in manufacturing and mining completed in the 1974–76 period and found that the acquiring firms were buying firms with stronger rates of growth of sales revenues; in fact, the weaker the sales growth rate of the acquiring company, the stronger that of the acquired company. He also found that the acquiring firm had lower rates of return on assets and a tendency to acquire firms whose returns on assets were higher than theirs, as if to maintain a level of profitability by acquisition.[6] Some part of this

5 Ronald W. Melicher and David F. Rush, 'Evidence on the Acquisition-Related Performance of Conglomerate Firms', *Journal of Finance*, 29(1) (March 1974), 141–9.
6 Jae H. Song, 'Diversifying Acquisition and Financial Relationships: Testing 1974–1976 Behavior', *Strategic Management Journal*, 4(2) (April–June 1983), 97–108.

activity could be explained as a process by which to obtain optimal financial leverage. As indicated by Lewellen[7] and Lintner,[8] an acquiring firm may have had 'latent' debt capacity which could be used to finance the acquisition of a less levered firm. As a result of the acquisition, the acquiring firm uses the acquired's potential to borrow. This explanation, however, did not answer the question as to why it was not equally or more effective simply to issue debt and buy back shares in the existing enterprise, without undertaking the transactions cost involved in a takeover. Weston and Mansinghka[9] argued that many corporations entered into the conglomeration process through merger as a financial strategy, involving removing assets from existing markets and operations with depressed earnings and placing them in higher earnings opportunities elsewhere. This again is a diversification strategy that may or may not be profit-maximizing, or even derived from a profit motive, since the basic test for profitability is whether the acquired companies offer a higher return prospect to the investors in the acquiring corporations than investments for the shareholder after paying out higher dividends or buying back shares.

The more persuasive argument was provided by Dennis Mueller's 'A Theory of Conglomerate Mergers' published in 1969.[10] His position was that merger history demonstrated that 'managers maximize the growth in physical size of their corporation rather than their profits or stockholder welfare'.[11] He went on to argue that a wealth of behavioural evidence indicated that the financial rewards which managers received were tied to growth of their companies, not to earnings for investors. He states:

> managerial salaries, bonuses, stock options and promotions tend to be more closely related to the size, or the changes in size, of the firm than to its profits. Similarly the prestige and power that managers derive from their occupations are directly related to the size and growth of the company and not to its profitability.[12]

---

7  Wilber G. Lewellen, 'A Pure Financial Rationale for the Conglomerate Merger', *Journal of Finance* (May 1971), 521–37.

8  John Lintner, 'Expectations, Mergers and Equilibrium in Purely Competitive Securities Markets', *American Economic Review* (May 1971), 101–11.

9  J. Fred Weston and Surenda K. Mansinghka, 'Test of the Efficiency Performance of Conglomerate Firms', *Journal of Finance* (September 1971), 919–36.

10  Dennis C. Mueller, 'A Theory of Conglomerate Mergers', *Quarterly Journal of Economics*, 83(4) (November 1969), 643–59.

11  Ibid., 644.

12  Ibid.

While Mueller was unable to test this hypothesis, he did survey the merger history of that time to 'make some judgment' as to whether the growth maximization hypothesis was more plausible. He found that mergers in 1966 were proceeding at roughly nine times the rate that had immediately preceded the Second World War and 2½ times the level of the 1946–47 high merger period. The dollar value of the assets of acquired firms increased between 1951 and 1966 from $201 million to over $4 billion, with most of that increase consisting of assets in conglomerate mergers. Most relevant to his hypothesis was the finding that the proportion of firm growth from mergers was higher the larger the firm. The tendency of large firms to grow more from merger implied that growth maximization was the goal in that period. Considering the alternative, Mueller found it implausible that 'managers with no familiarity with the company's operations could recognize its opportunity for profits better than the firm's own managers and stockholders'.[13]

By the late 1980s, investors had begun to recognize that responsibility for corporate behaviour that conflicted with their interest lay with managers who were not sufficiently focused on increasing earnings. The largest investors, in large part, began to turn to the board of directors. By the late 1980s, institutional investors – primarily public pension funds – had begun to demand publicly that, over and above advising and supporting management, boards hold managers accountable for merger and other aspects of performance.[14] As shareholders they had come to expect that directors of major corporate institutions would critically analyse the results of a year's operations and hold management responsible. These expectations were heightened through a series of well-publicized court cases brought against management and the directors.[15] In response, in the words of Chancellor William T. Allen who oversaw many of those cases in the Delaware Chancery Court, 'a lot of "soft" concepts like reputation, pride, fellowship and self-respect' would ideally bring directors, with prodding, to fulfil their duties and complete their assigned task.[16]

This was in effect a call for a return to basic governance doctrine: the board, as the shareholders' agent, would monitor management, causing management to focus on total returns to shareholders. That is, the

---

13  Ibid., 659.
14  Ira M. Millstein, speech to Council of Institutional Investors (CII) (1987) (on file with authors).
15  See note 23 below.
16  Letter from William T. Allen, Chancellor, Delaware Court of Chancery, to Ira M. Millstein (7 January 1993) (on file with the authors).

board would require that management develop operations that used resources to maximize earnings from the revenue product created which in turn would provide sustainable levels of payments to employees, material suppliers and others for services rendered. Those operations should be continued as long as earnings after taxes and interest at least equal the costs of equity investment (i.e., equal to the returns generated by alternative investments of equal risk in other organizations).

The board would ensure that management focused on the corporate polestar of maximizing corporate profit and shareholder gain. When the earnings margin, equal to revenues minus operating costs, is optimized, then as a conceptual matter operations have the best chance of continuing at an efficient scale. In most cases, following this operating rule reduces outlays to favoured stakeholders and increases returns to investors, whether in cash disbursements or increased new investment. This allocation of earnings to dividends or to increases in capital outlays spurs the corporation's efficient and profitable growth. This is what many large investors saw as happening in the 1980s: corporate turn arounds to positions of advantage in world manufacturing.

In effect, history shows that governance mattered – or that it was supposed to matter. In the 1970s and 1980s, it was made apparent that weak governance was associated with declines in both earnings performance and in the corporation's position within its industry. So-called 'managerial capitalism', by which managers bypassed boards of directors, focussed on employee problems, community enhancements, and/or strategies to perpetuate the corporation rather than efficiency gains to increase returns on investment had not prevailed.[17]

With conglomeration, those practising managerial capitalism were spread more broadly, and in many ways thinner, across the product landscape. Performance of US corporations declined relative to that of German and Japanese corporations operating under different systems of governance.[18] The American conglomerate corporation produced lower

---

17 For the classic description of the rise of the professional manager in the USA, see generally Alfred D. Chandler, Jr, *The Visible Hand: The Managerial Revolution in American Business* (1977). As other commentators have noted, in the post-Second World War era professional managers were 'virtually deified' by scholars such as Chandler and Peter F. Ducker, while the role of the board was virtually ignored. See, e.g., James Gillies, *Boardroom Renaissance: Power, Morality and Performance in the Modern Corporation* (1992), 4–7 (describing how boards were viewed as a legal fiction).

18 Carol J. Loomis, 'Dinosaurs?', *Fortune*, 3 May 1993, 36.

quality, and less innovative, products, limiting the opportunity for profitable additional investment.

We use the conglomerate example as a surrogate for weak boards allowing management's self interest to dominate in disregard of shareholder value. Management's interest in size and scope, as distinguished from shareholder value, led other major icons not classified as conglomerates to serious decline. As we observed in our *Columbia Law Review* article:

> By the early 1990s, many of the largest corporations were faltering. For example, IBM, General Motors, and Sears – which, in 1972, had respectively ranked first, fourth, and sixth in the world in total value of outstanding shares – were no longer represented in the 1992 top twenty largest companies, ranked by stock value. Together they had reportedly lost a total of $32.4 billion of market valuation in 1992 alone.[19]

These three companies went through a cycle that was to be repeated by many other large manufacturing enterprises. With management-dominated strategies the corporations had invested in low-return growth and diversification to expand the size and scope of core activities.[20] The resulting low-level returns to investors had begun to put boards under increasing pressure from: (i) institutional shareholders, primarily the large public pension funds;[21] (ii) takeover

---

19  I. Millstein and P. MacAvoy, 'The Active Board of Directors and Performance of the Large Publicly Traded Corporation', *Columbia Law Review*, 98 (June 1998), 1,283, 1,285 (citing Loomis, 'Dinosaurs?', 36, 36–7). A dominant managerial system acting without true accountability was held partially to blame.

20  Millstein and MacAvoy, 'The Active Board', 1,285 (citing Loomis, 'Dinosaurs?', at 39–41).

21  See, e.g., 'Thinking More About Institutions', *Institutional Investor* (November 1990), 176 (survey of 700 investor relations officers, finding that the courting of institutional investors has never been more intense); Amy L. Goodman, 'Institutional Investors Come of Age', *Insights*, 4(2) (December 1990) (reporting that an assembly of 100 private institutional money managers, who had in the past been prepared to sell rather than vote against management, were now focused on proxy activism and shareholder rights); CalPERS, *Company Responses to Request for Board Governance Self-Evaluation – Final Report* (May 1995) (CalPERS' survey and scorecard of the corporate governance practices of the 300 largest companies in its portfolio); Russell Reynolds Associates and The Wirthlin Group, *Redefining Corporate Governance: 1995 U.S. Survey of Institutional Investors*, 3–7 (finding increased investor activism prompts changes in board composition, compensation and activism); Wirthlin Worldwide and

firms;[22] and (iii) judicial interpretations of fiduciary duties.[23] In addition, public attacks by noted Delaware jurists raised directors' concerns for

---

Russell Reynolds Associates, *Setting New Standards For Corporate Governance: 1997 U.S. Survey of Institutional Investors*, 3 (corporate governance examination was given 'impetus by a number of high-profile cases that demonstrated what could happen when boards were insufficiently vigilant in their oversight duties'); Stuart L. Gillan and Laura T. Starks, 'A Survey of Shareholder Activism: Motivation and Empirical Evidence', *Contemporary Finance Digest*, 2 (Autumn 1998), 10–34 (finding that as the equity ownership of investment advisers, investment companies, bank trust departments, insurance companies, foundations and pension funds increased from 24 per cent of the market in 1980 to just under 50 per cent by the end of 1994, they became more active participants in the governance of their corporate holdings); and Gillan and Starks, 'Corporate Governance Proposals and Shareholder Activism: The Role of Institutional Investors', *Journal of Financial Economics*, 57 (2000), 275–305 (an empirical study of increased shareholder activism on the part of institutional investors over the past 15 years).

22 See, e.g., Michael J. Barclay and Clifford G. Holderness, 'Control of Corporations by Active Block Investors', *Journal of Applied Corporate Finance* (Fall 1991), 68 (study of 106 block trades of common stock during 1978–1982, finding 'considerable evidence that block purchasers or their representatives play an active role in firm management' and that 'turnover among top managers and directors after the trades substantially exceeded what is normal for public corporations').

23 A series of Delaware court decisions in the 1980s concerning the contours of the business judgment rule in the context of board response to a change of control situation emphasized the role of informed independent directors. See *Paramount Communications, Inc.* v. *Time Inc.*, 571 A.2d 1,140, 1,150–1 Del. Ch. (Del. 1990) (holding board had no duty to maximize shareholder value where there was no evidence that by negotiating with merger partner, dissolution or break up of company was inevitable), affirming 1989 WL 79880, at 19 (14 July 1989) (*'Delaware law does recognize that directors, when acting deliberately, in an informed way, and in the good faith pursuit of corporate interests, may follow a course designed to achieve long-term value even at the cost of immediate value maximization'*: emphasis in original); *Mills Acquisition Co.* v. *MacMillan, Inc.*, 559 A.2d 1,261, 1,279–80 (Del. 1989) (board breached fiduciary duty by delegating sale process to self-interested CEO and CFO (Chief Financial Officer), who deliberately concealed material information from the board); *Ivanhoe Partners* v. *Newmont Mining Corp.*, 535 A.2d 1,334, 1,341, 1,343 (Del. 1987) (presence of independent directors comprising majority of board members that voted on merger enhanced proof that board acted in informed good faith); *Revlon, Inc.* v. *MacAndrews & Forbes Holdings, Inc.*, 506 A.2d 173, 182 (Del. 1986) (when break-up of the company becomes inevitable 'directors' role changed from defenders of the corporate bastion to auctioneers charged with getting the best price for the stockholders'); *Moran* v. *Household Int'l, Inc.*, 500 A.2d 1,346, 1,356 (Del. 1985) (independent directors exercised informed

their own reputations and performance.[24] The response was often late in arriving, and sometimes too late to prevent irreversible decline.

## Other Sources of accelerated change

Corporate poor performance led to misconduct in some, quite spectacular examples of failed governance. In the early 1970s, the SEC launched an investigation of Penn Central Railroad:[25] 'the Enron failure of its day'.[26] The SEC criticized the Penn Central board for failing to oversee the company's operations, for lacking independence from management, and for being unable to identify the company's financial problems.[27]

---

business judgment in adopting poison pill shareholder rights plan); *Unocal Corp. v. Mesa Petroleum Co.*, 493 A.2d 946, 953–55 (Del. 1985) (whether directors' actions taken in response to a perceived threat are reasonable in relation to the threat posed is 'materially enhanced' where board is comprised of majority of independent directors); see generally Dennis J. Block, Nancy E. Barton and Stephen A. Radin, *The Business Judgment Rule: Fiduciary Duties of Corporate Directors* (5th ed. 1998 and Supp. 2002), 823–32 (discussing the impact of Delaware court decisions with respect to the role of outside directors and special committees); Robert A. Ragazzo, 'Unifying the Law of Hostile Takeovers: The Impact of QVC and its Progeny', *Houston Law Review*, 32 (1995), 945, 976 (tracing evolution of judicial definition of board duties).

24  See memorandum from William T. Allen, Chancellor, Delaware Court of Chancery, to the 1993 Tulane Corporate Law Institute (undated), 11 (on file with the authors) (discussing the role of '"soft" concepts like reputation, pride, fellowship and self-respect' in motivating directors to become more active); William T. Allen, Chancellor, Delaware Court of Chancery, 'Redefining the Role of Outside Directors in an Age of Global Competition', Speech at Ray Garrett, Jr, Corporate and Securities Law Institute, Northwestern University (30 April 1992), in Robert A.G. Monks and Nell Minow, *Corporate Governance*, app. 4 at 494 (1995) ('For the most part the men and women who sit on the boards ... want to do the right thing in that job. They want to deserve the respect of the communities from which they are drawn'); see also Ira M. Millstein, 'The Evolution of the Certifying Board', *Business Lawyer*, 48 (1993), 1,485, 1,488.

25  Abstract of article, *The New York Times*, 7 August 1972, 1 (SEC announced investigation of 15 former officers of Penn Central in connection with their sale of stock based on inside information and failure to disclose financial information, just prior to the collapse of the stock's value).

26  *Accounting and Investor Protection Issues Raised by Enron and Other Public Companies: Hearing Before the Senate Comm. on Banking, Housing, and Urban Affairs*, 107th Cong. 2 (2002) (statement by Charles A. Bowsher, Chairman, Public Oversight Board).

27  Ibid.

Following the Penn Central investigation, the SEC began to focus on financial reporting and board oversight of management in a number of other corporations. While the link between Penn Central and SEC focus on audit procedures was not totally clear in its enforcement actions, the SEC in general began to require that boards form committees, composed wholly of independent directors, designed to monitor compliance with SEC regulations on financial reporting.[28] Then, in 1977, the SEC approved a New York Stock Exchange rule requiring all listed US companies to form audit committees comprised of a majority of independent directors.[29] The new listing rule marked the beginning

---

28 In response to legal action by the SEC against Gulf Oil Corp. for alleged political payoffs, the Gulf board formed a special committee to report on Gulf's internal state: see Allan J. Mayer, 'Washington Money-Go-Round', *Newsweek* (8 December 1975, 71). Following release of company financial statements that revealed misstatements of sales and incomes, the SEC petitioned a Federal Court in 1974 to require Mattel, Inc. to name a majority of independent directors to its board (Felix Belair Jr, Abstract of article, *The New York Times*, 3 October 1974, 61) and, in settling a civil fraud action against Mattel for improper financial reporting, forced the toy manufacturer to establish two special board committees, one on financial controls and auditing, the other on litigation and claims. see Christopher D. Stone, 'Public Directors Merit a Try', *Harvard Business Review* (March–April 1976), 20. As part of a settlement with the SEC in 1975 regarding illegal political payments in the USA and abroad and the filing of false reports, Ashland Oil Inc. was required to form a special board committee to investigate and report on their findings: see 'Ashland Political Payments Made Abroad, Facts on File', *World News Digest*, 19 July 1975, 514 B1. See generally 'End of the Directors' Rubber Stamp', *Business Week*, 10 September 1979, 72 *et seq*.

> Nowhere is the emergence of the activist board more evident than in the creation of various working committees. The idea of boardroom committees goes back more than three decades, but as recently as the mid-1970s, only a small fraction of corporate boards had standing committees composed mostly of outside directors...Most government pressure for more responsible boards...has been coming from the SEC, which lately has dramatically stepped up investigations into director negligence or misconduct.

29 'What you Can and Cannot Do if you Run a Business', *U.S. News and World Report*, 28 March 1977, 80 (reporting that SEC approved the proposed NYSE rule requiring all domestic companies with NYSE-listed common stock to set up majority independent audit committees by 1 July 1978). The NYSE rule was amended in 1999 to require that all audit committee members be independent: 'Each audit committee shall consist of at least three directors, all of whom have no relationship to the company that may interfere with the exercise of their independence from management and the company': NYSE, *Listed Company Manual*, § 303.01(B)(2)(a) (December 1999).

of the emergence of independent directors as a key component of governance change.[30]

The board's responsibilities gained further attention in the mid-1980s when the surge in corporate takeover activity, and related court actions, led the SEC to require boards to pursue the interests of investors seeking to sell their shares to acquiring firms when management resisted a takeover.[31] The SEC made board positions contestable when it revised the proxy rules for voting shares in annual board elections to allow shareholders to join together and publicize their voting positions against a management initiative.[32] With increasing sophistication in the use of shareholder power – and recognition of their limited ability to sell the stock of under-performing portfolio companies – key institutional investors began to work to improve the accountability of corporate managers.

Finally, the decision by the General Motors (GM) board to publish 'governance guidelines' after it had discharged a non-performing CEO – and the decision by CalPERS to ask its portfolio companies whether they had considered adopting guidelines similar to the GM guidelines – brought the issue of governance and corporate performance to the attention of all large US corporations.[33]

At the same time, the most important first step in 'reform' governance, board independence, was becoming encouraged and legitimized by courts – principally in Delaware – that set forth new rules for governance authority and responsibility. In a series of now famous cases, the Delaware courts made it clear that boards could and should determine key strategic decisions, acting independently of management, through a thoughtful

---

30 By the early 1980s, 70 per cent of the 1,000 largest US corporations possessed boards composed of a majority of outside directors; 97 per cent had boards with audit committees composed of a majority of outside directors; 80 per cent had executive committees (responsible for monitoring management) with majorities of outside directors, and 37 per cent had nominating committees with a majority of outside directors. See 'End of the Directors' Rubber Stamp', 72 *et seq.* (referencing a Korn/Ferry International survey).

31 See *Unocal Corp.* v. *Mesa Petroleum Co.*, 493 A.2d 946 (Del. 1985).

32 See 17 C.F.R. parts 228, 229, 240, 249 (1992).

33 Millstein and MacAvoy, 'The Active Board', 1,283, 1,289–90; CalPERS, *Company Responses*; General Motors Board of Directors, *GM Board of Directors Corporate Governance Guidelines on Significant Corporate Governance Issues* (January 1994, subsequently revised). See discussion, Ch. 4, note 9.

and diligent decision-making process.[34] In addition, the courts gave responsibility to boards of directors to evaluate tender offers to determine whether a takeover was best for the corporation's shareholders.[35] Failure to 'exercise a duty of care' when the sale of the company was involved put board members at risk of liability for shareholder losses.[36] These cases established the responsibility of the board for the corporation's long-term goals, and strategy, as well as for approval of management's plans to achieve such a strategy. If the directors were 'informed' and 'diligent', a board recommendation to investors to accept or reject a tender offer for the company would be given deference by the courts.[37]

These judicial clarifications not only informed directors of their prerogatives, but also of how they were to act if their decisions were to be confirmed in what inevitably became legal proceedings. The cases

---

34 See *Paramount Communications, Inc.*, 571 A.2d 1,154 (holding board had no duty to maximize shareholder value where break-up of company was not inevitable and majority of directors were independent and adequately informed), aff'g 1989 WL 79880 (Del. Ch. 14 July 1989); *Grobow* v. *Perot*, 539 A.2d 180, 188–92 (Del. 1988) (independent and informed directors properly exercised business judgment in approving repurchase of stock of director and largest shareholder); *Hanson Trust PLC* v. *SCM Acquisition, Inc.*, 781 F.2d 264, 275 (2d Cir. 1986) (enjoining exercise of lock-up option granted to one bidder because 'paucity of information and [directors'] swiftness of decision-making strongly suggests a breach of the duty of due care'); *Moran*, 500 A.2d 1,356 (independent directors exercised informed business judgment in adopting poison pill shareholder rights plan); *Smith v. Van Gorkom*, 488 A.2d 874 (directors have duty to act in informed and deliberate manner in determining whether to approve merger).

35 See *Unocal Corp.*, 493 A.2d 953–55 (board had power and duty to oppose tender offer where majority of independent directors acting in good faith and after reasonable investigation determined that proposal was inadequate, coercive and not in best interests of shareholders).

36 *Van Gorkom*, 488 A.2d 874 (directors breached duty of care by agreeing to sell company without informing themselves of CEO's motive to support sale, not being aware of company's intrinsic value, and rushing their deliberations where circumstances were not exigent).

37 See *Ivanhoe Partners*, 535 A.2d 1,344 (holding that defensive plans adopted in response to hostile tender offer were reasonable in relation to threat to shareholders); *Moran*, 500 A.2d 1,356 (directors exercised informed business judgment in adopting poison pill shareholder rights plan); *Unocal Corp.*, 493 A.2d 959 (board properly rejected tender offer where majority of independent directors acting in good faith and after reasonable investigation concluded that proposal was inadequate, coercive and not in best interests of shareholders).

from this era taught us that directors should be informed, diligent, and free from conflicts and should act independently of management. These requirements are central not only to corporate takeovers, but apply to everyday reviews of management and company performance as well.

In the early 1990s, events at GM focused the attention of institutional investors, the business media and ultimately other corporate boards on the need for board activism and independence in the face of non-performing managers. With performance faltering and no satisfactory plan in place to stem the loss of market position, GM's board discharged the CEO in October 1992 and then began to consider how to ensure its own continued leadership. The remoulding of the governance structure began with the election of three new directors and the appointment of a non-executive member to the board chairmanship. The board's action was viewed as a watershed event. Indeed, the *Wall Street Journal* reporters who told the GM story as it unfolded won a Pulitzer Prize for their reporting.[38] Then in the spring of 1994, the GM board issued 28 guidelines designed to facilitate its ability, as an independent board, to actively discharge its responsibility to make sure that the resources of the corporation were used effectively.[39] Key provisions included:

- independent board leadership in the form of either a non-executive chairman or a lead independent director;
- regular meetings of the independent directors without management present to discuss CEO and management performance, and assess that performance against the strategic objectives of the company;
- governance structure and process determined by independent directors;
- annual board self-evaluation;
- selection of board member candidates by independent directors with input from the CEO.[40]

---

38  'Two Wall Street Journal Reporters Win Pulitzer for Coverage of GM's Turmoil', *Wall Street Journal*, 14 April 1993, A2. See Paul J. Ingrassia and Joseph B. White, *Comeback: The Fall and Rise of the American Automobile Industry* (Simon & Schuster, 1994), 277–321.

39  See Robert L. Simison, 'GM Board Adopts Formal Guidelines on Stronger Control Over Management', *Wall Street Journal*, 28 March 1994, A4.

40  See GM, *Corporate Governance Guidelines* 2, 7, 8, 9, 11, 15, 19, 20, 21, 25. These guidelines were consistent with the principles of board governance advocated by the Working Group on Corporate Governance, a coalition of lawyers for large public companies and leading institutional investors, and were published as 'A New Compact for Owners and Directors', *Harvard Business Review*, (July–August 1991), 41 *et seq.*

Aside from the publicity given to the issue, the guidelines were notable because they articulated a reform position in corporate governance by establishing the necessity of board independence and shifting authority on matters of strategy and executive tenure to the board and away from the executives themselves.

The GM board actions were widely discussed in the popular media, including the already mentioned *Wall Street Journal* coverage. *Business Week* christened GM's corporate governance document the 'Magna Carta for Directors'.[41] The basic practices making up 'active' board decision-making were publicly enumerated and calls for other boards to exert more leadership came from impeccable sources. The GM board acted in response to poor (but previously acceptable) management performance. The 'soft concepts' long held dormant were beginning to become effective responsibilities. Directors that would previously have fired management only after bankruptcy now acted earlier in order to revitalize corporate performance.[42]

Boards of other large corporations put this GM initiative to the test with high-profile renovations of their governance systems. During a two-week

41  Judith H. Dobrzynski, 'At GM, A Magna Carta for Directors', *Business Week*, 4 April 1994, 37.

42  Within a short time, the National Association of Corporate Directors (NACD) and the American Bar Association (ABA) published guidelines for various aspects of corporate governance. See *Report of the Blue Ribbon Commission on Performance Evaluation of Chief Executive Officers, Boards and Directors* (1994); ABA Committee on Corporate Laws, Section of Business Law, *Corporate Directors' Guidebook* (2nd edn 1994). See also *Report of the Committee on the Financial Aspects of Corporate Governance* (Cadbury Report) (December 1992, reissued April 1996, combined with other reports into publication by the London Stock Exchange (LSE), *Principles of Good Governance and Code of Best Practice (The Combined Code)*, 1998); Toronto Stock Exchange (TSE) Committee on Corporate Governance in Canada, *'Where Were The Directors?': Guidelines for Improved Corporate Governance in Canada* (Dey Report) (December 1994).

Numerous additional guidelines have issued in the past nine years from the business, investor and labour communities. See American Federation of Labor and Congress of Industrial Organizations (AFL-CIO), *Investing in Our Future: AFL-CIO Proxy Voting Guidelines* (1997); The Business Roundtable, *Statement of the Business Round Table on Corporate Governance* (September 1997), subsequently revised as *Statement of the Business Round Table on Corporate Governance Principles Relating to the Enron Bankruptcy* (February 2002); TIAA-CREF, *TIAA-CREF Policy Statement on Corporate Governance* (October 1997, subsequently revised); CII, *Core Policies, General Principles, Positions and Explanatory Notes* (March 1998); CalPERS, *Corporate Governance Core Principles and Guidelines: The United States* (April 1998).

period, in January 1993, the boards of three major US corporations took action in their oversight role to find and install new senior managers for what became known as 'that vision thing'[43] in order to restore previous high performance. Westinghouse's board changed its bylaws to empower itself to act, then accepted the CEO's resignation, installed one of its own as non-executive chairman, and started to search for a 'vision' leader. At IBM, the board first resisted stockholder pressure to remove a chairman/CEO unable to change the company's age-old culture, but eventually the board installed one of its members as non-executive chairman and began to search for a new CEO to redirect the company's immense resources and get going again. Both boards asserted themselves by discharging CEOs, not because of disastrous performance, but because their performance did not constitute the best that could be achieved.

Perhaps the most telling CEO ousting took place at American Express. After a highly public discussion as to whether the board should discharge the chairman/CEO, of whom the major shareholders no longer approved, the board decided that while he would be required to step down he would remain in some capacity. But then, according to press reports, a group of institutional shareholders objected to a management structure that did not clearly define who was to be the 'change agent' responsible for future performance. This time, the public pension funds did not complain; rather, unlikely shareholder activists such as J.P. Morgan Investment Management, Alliance Capital Management, Putnam Management and other institutions, which together owned 20 per cent of American Express common stock, pressed for change.[44] Following a breakfast meeting where this investor group registered its complaint, the chairman/CEO resigned, a member of the board assumed the non-executive chairmanship and the board installed a new CEO.

While other notable events took place during this period these three highly publicized board (and shareholder) initiatives put board activism (and the threat of shareholder activism) on the agenda of corporate leaders. These boards acted in response to messages delivered by large shareholders, in most cases concerned about failing share values in the

---

43  Michael W. Miller and Laurence Hooper, 'Signing Off', *Wall Street Journal*, 27 January 1993, A1, A6 (outsiders will search for a new chief executive to be a 'Change-Master').

44  Susan Pulliam and Steven Lipin, 'Some Major American Express Holders Voice Disappointment about Robinson', *Wall Street Journal*, 29 January 1993, A4.

stock market. These were examples of boards taking action with companies not in dire crisis, but simply unwilling to continue 'business as usual' when faced with falling market share and share prices. By taking the initiative and confronting management with the need for improvements in both strategic and programmatic leadership, passive governance became active and the board of directors began to act with true independence.

## The emergence of the full role of the board of directors

As governance changed during the early 1990s, arguments as to the increased authority and responsibility of the board of directors began to appear regularly in the business press. It was said that a directorship made ever-increasing time demands, left no room for amateurs, and required greater compensation for high-quality service. Monitoring of management had to be aimed at detecting and responding to performance problems before they developed into crises. The board's role had to expand beyond monitoring managers to more substantive areas, including strategic planning and providing incentives for managers that were linked to corporate performance. To a certain extent the business press called for these changes to take place soon, albeit through an evolutionary process.

Such a position was based on the concept of professionalism in the boardroom at the core of 'reformed' governance.[45] Senior management is responsible for the enterprise's efficiency, and thus its competitiveness. Boards of directors are responsible for hiring, compensating, monitoring and planning the succession of senior management. Viewed from this perspective, as fiduciaries for owners, boards are responsible, in effect, for the corporation's performance. Professionalism is the process of taking on and delivering upon that responsibility.

This more penetrating involvement in decision-making authority begins with participating in the formulation of corporate strategy. Typically, separate parts of the strategic plan are developed by senior management in each of the divisions, integrated by the CEO's staff and then framed for strategic focus by the CEO. The strategy is approved by the board or, if not, it is rejected and returned to management – a

---

45 Ira M. Millstein, 'The Professional Board', *The Business Lawyer*, August 1995; 'The Responsible Board', *The Business Lawyer*, February 1997; 'Director Professionalism', Report of the NACD Blue Ribbon Commission (1996, updated and reprinted 2001).

decision that would be regarded as showing disapproval of management conduct. When the plan is approved, it is implemented on a schedule to be determined by management. This process varies but, in the end, management has the primary responsibility for developing and articulating strategy, as well as the knowledge of operations necessary to execute the plan effectively in a competitive environment. Beyond approving or disapproving the management's proposal, the role of the board has been to set acceptable performance levels in reference to the strategic plan and then evaluate management accordingly.[46]

There has been growing boardroom interest in assuming a more active role in the strategic process.[47] If the board is to determine the merits of management's strategic and business plans, including the likelihood of realizing the intended results, then it should, at the very least, determine for itself the capacity of specific operations to generate the returns expected to be in keeping with the strategy. The board should be able to assess the strategies of existing and potential corporate rivals, and the impact that changes in the external environment – economic, social, and political – could have on performance under this strategy and that of rivals. This assessment should be grounded in a board consensus on the characteristics of the organization – its assets, liabilities, and structure – that affect performance.[48] These conditions require that the board be part of the strategy development process, in order to satisfy itself that management is proposing the preferred choice of a series of possible courses of action. The board should identify benchmarks that might indicate a change in expected results, such as developments that may take place (for example, in the market) after implementation of the plan has begun and may require that the plan be modified.

---

46  See, e.g., Gordon Donaldson, 'A New Tool for Boards: The Strategic Audit', *Harvard Business Review* (July–August 1995), 99; John Pound, 'Corporate Governance Affects Corporate Strategy', *Corporate Board* (July–August 1994), 1; C. Gopinath, J.I. Siciliane and R.L. Murray, 'Changing Role of the Board of Directors: In Search of a New Strategic Identity?', *Mid-Atlantic Journal of Business*, 30 (1994), 175; Allen, 'Redefining the Role', 30 April 1992. While strategic planning seems to be more of a developed science, it is suspected that the elements of board involvement in mission development are similarly fuzzy.

47  *Report of the NACD Blue Ribbon Commission on the Role of the Board in Corporate Strategy* (September 2000); *Report of the NACD Blue Ribbon Commission on Director Professionalism* (November 1996, reissued 2001).

48  Sharon Oster, *Modern Competitive Analysis* 5 (2nd edn, 1994).

Monitoring management performance based on strategic directives constitutes a major escalation of board activity. The board's monitoring function had been traditionally focused on management presentations of current month and quarter revenues and operating costs. This information has been presented by management in more detail, but at the same level of content, as contained in the corporation public financial statements. Accordingly, the information available to the directors has been more current, but certainly not more analytical, than that available to stock analysts. But this rendition of financial performance measures would not be sufficient for the board to monitor the corporation's long-term performance against the strategic plan; extrapolating monthly data series to generate forecasts of future performance does not allow the board to accurately anticipate problems to come. If the board is to evaluate corporate performance beyond the level achieved by the typical stock analyst it needs sharper tools and more information.

The need for tools for measuring plan performance seems obvious. If the plan calls for doubling the production of nuts and bolts, the board should have measures of nuts and bolts production; but if the plan calls for increasing market share, then the board should have accurate measures of market share not only in physical units but also in revenues and earnings. If the plan calls for 'becoming global', then the board must define the term and measure the elements of globalization that would be earnings-related. The board has to call for measurable performance elements, obtain the relevant information regularly, and then evaluate results in those terms. The board should not rely solely on historical data, or on how management describes its own performance in qualitative terms. It has to assess whether management has positioned itself for what may be coming in the next few market periods by assessing the strengths of forthcoming plans and programs in terms of their realism and implications.

Measuring the ability of management to produce future wealth in these terms requires a high order of sophistication. As recognized in the 1992 report of the Council on Competitiveness, a corporation's future depends on, among other things, its current stock of scientific and technical knowledge and its reputation with suppliers, customers and investors, as well as its present and future market competitive position.[49]

---

49 Council on Competitiveness, *Capital Choices: Changing the Way America Invests in Industry* (1992), 84; See also The Conference Board, *Commission on Public Trust and Enterprise: Findings and Recommendations* (2003).

A strong grasp of these indicators should be available to help the board in appraising the enterprise's future performance. Production rates and shipments (which indicate current status relative to order book inventories) and forecasts of sales based on informed and sophisticated assessments can be used to anticipate changes. Such data can be supplemented by industry-level forecasts of demand and capacity utilization. These data and estimates, together with price information, make it possible for the board to consider present value cash-flow projections of mainstream operations.

The board could also review and assess financial analyst appraisals of current and future performance. Analyst studies are responsive to interests of the investor, and rely on indicators of performance relevant to those interests, even though they are widely perceived to be biased in favor of selling shares. Whether forecasts of future performance from such sources are accurate enough to guide the board's assessment varies from case to case; but aligning its position against that of management, and also that of the analysts on near and long-term performance, could be the board's contribution.[50]

## Has the emergence of 'new' governance, in terms of board diligence and focus, become observable?

Surveys on the activism and focus of board/management relations are revealing. Korn/Ferry International reports the following information.

1  Two-thirds of respondents' boards (67 per cent) had a formal process for evaluating the CEO in 2001, the same percentage as in 1994.[51]
2  The number of directors who reported that their boards had full-board performance evaluations increased to 42 per cent in 2001 (up from 26 per cent in 1994).[52]

---

50  Following a submission to the NYSE and NASDAQ by the Blue Ribbon Committee on Improving the Effectiveness of Audit Committees, the NYSE and NASDAQ adopted new listing requirements that further institutionalized the role and independence of the audit committee *vis-à-vis* management. See Report and Recommendations of the Blue Ribbon Committee on Improving the Effectiveness of Corporate Audit Committees (Ira M. Millstein and John C. Whitehead, Co-chairman) (1999) and Securities and Exchange Release Nos. 34-42231 (NASD Rule making); and 34-2233 (NYSE Rule making).
51  Korn/Ferry International, *Board Meeting in Session: 23rd Annual Board of Directors Study* (1996), 25; Korn/Ferry, *28th Annual Board of Directors Study* (2001), 20.
52  Korn/Ferry, *23rd Annual Board Study*, 28; *28th Annual Board of Directors Study*, 22.

3 Seventy-five per cent of directors reported that their boards had written guidelines on corporate governance in 2001 (up from 59 per cent in 1995, the first year this aspect was reported in this survey).[53]

Similarly, a National Association of Corporate Directors (NACD) survey in 2001 found that board independence and the board's participation in strategy formulation had increased. Moreover, according to the survey, boards were undertaking more rigorous CEO and self-evaluations.[54] The Conference Board's 1996 study, *The Corporate Board: A Growing Role in Strategic Assessment*, documented recognition of the legitimacy of board involvement in strategy formulation. In a ten-country study, 51 per cent of respondents stated that their boards had a greater role in strategy than they did three years earlier, and nearly 49 per cent stated that the board was 'actively engaged in the choice of strategic options'.[55] By the end of the century, then, it seemed that 'professionalism' in the boardroom was structurally coming into place. Was it also beginning to determine conduct?

Before finding the answer we first examine whether strong governance–with professionalism-dominating board practice – results in better corporate performance (in Chapters 4 and 5). Is governance reform worth the effort?

---

53 Korn/Ferry, *23rd Annual Board Study*, 27; *28th Annual Board of Directors Study*, 22.

54 NACD, *Public Company Governance Survey*, November 2001, 7–9, 18–19.

55 The Conference Board, *The Corporate Board: A Growing Role in Strategic Assessment* (1996), 12. An NACD report released prior to the corporate governance scandals of 2001 and 2002 urged that boards should be 'constructively engaged' with management to ensure the appropriate development, execution, and modification of the company's strategy. See the *NACD Blue Ribbon Commission Report on the Role of the Board in Corporate Strategy*, September 2000, *passim*.

# 4

# The Ambivalent Results of Extant Research on the Impact of Strong Governance on Corporate Performance

*Ira M. Millstein and Paul W. MacAvoy*

The 'effectiveness' of boards has been the subject of numerous investigations by analysts and financial experts. They have not resulted in a consensus position. The studies have centred on major events such as corporate takeovers, restructurings, or replacements of the CEO. A substantial body of work has developed regarding the relationship of these events, and how they were addressed in the context of corporate governance. But this body of work has been too narrowly focused for any general findings on the governance performance relationship. The initial difficulty in generating conclusive empirical results stems from the failure to develop a proxy for board 'independence'. Most studies have relied on some measure of board composition, such as the number of outside versus inside directors, to indicate 'independence'.[1] However, on their face, these surrogates are not associated with reform practices and shed little light on the conduct of an independent board.

---

1 We use the term 'outside' or 'non-executive' director to refer only to those directors that are not employees or executives of the firm. We use the term 'inside' to refer to employee or affiliated directors. We use the term 'independent' to refer to outside directors who lack family and business ties to the corporation.

We believe that because of the importance of personal interaction in the activity of a board, the simple tallying of the affiliations of individual board members provides insufficient information to assess whether or not that board is active and independent. This position, that director independence is more complex than a listing of affiliations would indicate, is supported by Shivdasani and Yermack, who found that the CEO's involvement in the selection of directors negatively affected the independence and quality of the nominee.[2] An accurate appraisal of board independence is not based simply on the composition of the board, but on observations of the board taking specific actions and following certain rules of practice.

However, the difficulty has been that of isolating observable determinants of behaviour. Agrawal and Knoeber identify seven mechanisms for control, including: shareholdings of insiders, institutions, and large block holders; observable authority of outside directors; corporate debt policy constraints; the managerial labour market; and the market for corporate control.[3] They find substantial interdependence among these determinants in a large sample of firms, but suggest that using one of these control sources to explain some measure of firm performance would be misleading. Similarly, Rediker and Seth found that there were strong substitution effects present among various aspects of governance conduct. They identified substitution between monitoring by outside directors and large shareholders, as well as monitoring by inside directors in determining the performance of management.[4]

Of central concern, however, are incentives to actively monitor management in the interest of shareholders. Much research has focused on determining adequate incentives for directors to develop a strong governance system.[5] The authors of these papers acknowledge that directors

---

2 See Anil Shivdasani and David Yermack, 'CEO Involvement in the Selection of New Board Members: An Empirical Analysis', *Journal of Finance*, 54 (1999), 1,829–54.

3 See Anup Agrawal and Charles R. Knoeber, 'Firm Performance and Mechanisms to Control Agency Problems between Managers and Shareholders', *Journal of Financial and Quantative Analysis*, 31 (1996) 377–8.

4 Kenneth J. Rediker and Anju Seth, 'Boards of Directors and Substitution Effects of Alternative Governance Mechanisms', *Strategic Management Journal*, 16 (1995), 97–8.

5 See E. Fama, 'Agency Problems and the Theory of the Firm', *Journal of Political Economics*, 88 (1980), 288–307; E. Fama and Michael Jensen, 'Separation of Ownership and Control', *Journal of Law and Economics*, 26 (1983), 301–25.

respond to both monetary and non-monetary incentives, such as reputation, increased networking opportunities and forms of psychic income. On the other hand, having a reputation for being a director that does not make trouble for CEOs can be potentially valuable as well.[6]

One set of events in which setting appropriate director incentives is imperative is in board decisions on takeover proposals. Harford finds that directors of targeted companies who are likely to lose that particular board seat following the takeover are also less likely to acquire additional seats on other boards in the future.[7] With the expectation that a takeover will result in a loss of income and position for individual directors, Harford suggests that bonuses similar to management 'golden parachutes' should be employed to incentivize directors to be receptive to takeover bids. But more relevant than severance packages is the compensation directors receive during their tenure on the board; the compensation package can be constructed in a way that neutralizes the bias against takeovers. Director stock ownership, rather than monetary compensation, has been widely proposed as being important for aligning director and shareholder interests. Indeed, a shift to stock awards has been taking place; from 1992 to 1995 in a sample of large firms, the percentage with incentive-based compensation for directors rose from 48 per cent to 70 per cent. By 1995 such stock-based awards accounted for over one-third of total director compensation.[8] Significant correlation has been found between the amount of stock owned by outside directors and firm performance (based on a variety of measures). Higher share ownership of both corporate insiders and outside directors also has a positive correlation with both earnings performance and market value of the company's common shares.[9] Taken together, these studies indicate that director stock ownership may be used to align director and shareholder interests.

---

6 Benjamin E. Hermalin and Michael S. Weisbach, 'Boards of Directors as Endogenously Chosen Institutions: A Survey of the Economic Literature', unpublished manuscript available at http://www.nber.org/papers/w8161 (posted March 2001).

7 Jarrad Harford, 'Takeover Bids and Target Directors' Incentives: Retention, Experience and Settling-Up', *University of Oregon Working Paper* (2000).

8 See Tod Perry, 'Incentive Compensation for Outside Directors and CEO Turnover', working paper available at http://papers.ssrn.com (July 2000).

9 See Sanjai Bhagat, Dennis C. Carey and Charles M. Elson, 'Director Ownership, Corporate Performance, and Management Turnover', *Business Lawyer*, 54 (1999), 885.

There are other steps that have been taken to motivate the new 'strong governance'. There is evidence that small board size may be an element of effective corporate governance. Yermack reports in a recent article[10] that there is a significant negative correlation between board size and Tobin's $q$ (stock market value divided by the replacement value of assets); and Barnhart and Rosenstein confirm those results.[11] In other new research on CEO–chairman duality, however, there have been mixed results. Of four recent analyses of the separation of CEO and chairman, two find improved corporate performance, while the other two find no effect on performance. In the first study by Brickley, Coles and Jarrell, stock market valuation does not differ between samples of firms with split and consolidated CEO and chairman roles.[12] Similarly, Baliga, Moyer and Rao report no significant stock price effects from such an announcement, and no improvement in long-term earnings performance.[13] These studies are both based on the premise that current stock prices reflect past board behaviour, which is problematic.

On the other hand, Pi and Timme report that banks having non-chairman CEOs with large stock ownership have higher returns on assets.[14] Further, Rechner and Dalton report better performance for split position firms,[15] that splitting the roles of CEO and chairman leads to a more effective board.

Shareholder activism as a process for improving board and thus corporate performance has been widely recommended. Pressure has been applied by institutional investors from time to time to improve board

10 David Yermack, 'Higher Market Valuation of Companies with a Small Board of Director', *Journal of Financial Economics*, 40 (1996), 195, 202.

11 Scott W. Barnhart and Stuart Rosenstein, 'Board Composition, Managerial Ownership, and Firm Performance: An Empirical Analysis', *Financial Review*, 33 (1998), 11–12.

12 See James A. Brickley, Jeffery L. Coles and Gregg Jarrell, 'Leadership Structure: Separating the CEO and Chairman of the Board', *Journal of Corporate Finance*, 3 (1997), 189.

13 B. Ram Baliga, R. Charles Moyer and Ramesh S. Rao, 'CEO Duality and Firm Performance: What's All the Fuss?', *Strategic Management Journal*, 17 (1996), 41.

14 L. Pi and S.G. Timme, 'Corporate Control and Bank Efficiency', *Banking and Finance*, 17 (1993), 515.

15 Paula L. Rechner and Dan R. Dalton, 'CEO Duality and Organizational Performance: A Longitudinal Analysis', *Strategic Management Journal*, 12 (1991), 155.

structure and achieve board independence.[16] Many observers see such activism as ultimately improving investor returns; nonetheless, Roberta Romano concludes that such activities have had little or no effect on targeted firms' performance and that investors would be well served if they moved their attention elsewhere.[17] In her report, she concludes, 'for a large portion of the governance structures that are the focus of shareholder activism, such as independent boards of directors, limits on executive compensation, and confidential proxy voting, there is a paucity or utter absence of data that demonstrates that such devices improve performance'.[18]

Bernard Black is similarly negative about the impact of investor activism on firm performance, concluding that American shareholder activism to date has had 'little effect on firm performance'.[19] However, where Romano sees these efforts as ineffective due to the pursuit of unproven and inherently ineffective initiatives to achieve board independence, Black takes the position that ineffectiveness is due to the fact that these initiatives are simply too limited to have any real impact, noting that in general, 'they don't conduct proxy fights and don't try to elect their own candidates to the board of directors'.[20]

These legal studies are in contrast to recent empirical studies on the behaviour of large pension plans. CalPERS and four other similar funds sponsored 18 per cent of all corporate governance proposals submitted between 1987 and 1993. These efforts have had a significant effect on targeted firm governance.[21] Carleton, Nelson and Weisbach analysed correspondence between TIAA-CREF and 45 firms contacted regarding governance 'faults' identified between 1992 and 1996. During this period TIAA-CREF was able, either through private negotiation or

---

16  See, generally, Diane Del Guercio and Jennifer Hawkins, 'The Motivation and Impact of Pension Fund Activism', *Journal of Financial Economics*, 52 (1999), 293, 295, 297.

17  Roberta Romano, 'Less is More: Making Institutional Investor Activism a Valuable Mechanism of Corporate Governance', working paper available via http//:papers.ssrn.com (2000).

18  Romano, 'Less is More', 7. The report is marred by highlighting those studies that agree with her premise in the text and burying those that disagree in the footnotes.

19  See Bernard S. Black, 'Shareholder Activism and Corporate Governance in the United States', in Peter Newman (ed.), *The New Palgrave Dictionary of Economics and The Law* (Palgrave, 1998).

20  Ibid.

21  Del Guercio and Hawkins, 'Motivation and Impact', 293, 295, 297.

proxy vote, to reach agreement with 42 of the targeted companies.[22] Further recent evidence exists of the impact of shareholder activism regarding governance issues. The emergence of active institutional investors such as TIAA-CREF is associated with firms reducing board size and the proportion of inside directors.[23] But this process is aimed at forcing the boards of directors to act, rather than releasing them from management control so that they become independent and active boards.

Our position is that the empirical evidence seems to suggest, contrary to Black and Romano, that reform efforts are having some impact on current governance practice. While this does not negate Romano's claim that such efforts have not affected firm performance, a critical evaluation of the studies upon which her opinions are based is warranted.[24] Most institutional investor efforts are conducted in private so that studies of public data are biased, having been based on only those instances where private negotiations failed. In other words, the data is marred by a classic selection bias. And, finally, the empirical research has uncovered some correlation between performance and board activism. For example, Cotter, Shivdasani and Zenner found that tender offer targets with majority outsider boards realized approximately 20 per cent higher stock price returns between 1989 and 1992 than targets without such boards.[25] This finding is ambivalent, since targets with outsider boards should have higher offer prices because they are better managed, but acquirers with strong governance should offer a higher

---

22  Willard T. Carleton, James M. Nelson and Michael S. Weisbach, 'The Influence of Institutions on Corporate Governance through Private Negotiations: Evidence from TIAA-CREF', *Journal of Finance*, 53 (1998), 1,336.

23  Yilin Wu, 'Honey, CalPERS Shrunk the Board', working paper, University of Chicago (2000), available via http://papers.ssrn.com.

24  Studies cited in Romano's paper pertinent to this question include: James M. Forjan, 'The Wealth Effects of Shareholder-Sponsored Proposals', *Revised Financial Economics*, 8 (1999), 61–72 (finding a negative wealth effect for shareholder-sponsored proposals at a large number of firms); Jonathan Karpoff, Paul Malatesta and Ralph Walkling, 'Corporate Governance and Shareholder Initiatives: Empirical Evidence', *Journal of Financial Economics*, 42 (1996), 365–95 (finding evidence that targeted firm operating performance improves following shareholder proxy proposals); Sunil Wahal, 'Pension Fund Activism and Firm Performance', *Journal of Financial Quantitative Analysis*, 31 (1996), 1–23 (reporting no significant long-term stock price or accounting performance effect following pension fund shareholder proposals).

25  See James F. Cotter, Anil Shivdasani and Marc Zenner, 'Do Independent Directors Enhance Target Shareholder Wealth During Tender Offers?', *Journal of Financial Economics*, 43 (1997), 195.

takeover price premium to targets with insider boards for the opposite reason. Shareholders receive a higher premium in management buyouts if the firm has a majority of outsiders on its board.[26] Tender offer bidders with a majority of outsiders on the board earn roughly zero price returns on average, while bidders without such boards suffer statistically significant losses on average. This appears to be because bidders with a majority of outsiders on the board offer lower takeover premia, thereby preventing a final bid subject to the curse of paying too much.[27]

Regarding takeover defences, a number of studies find no significant correlation between the proportion of outside directors and the likelihood that the board will engage in takeover defences.[28] When firms adopt poison pill defences, the stock market reaction is significantly positive if the firm has a board consisting of a majority of outside directors, and significantly negative if it does not.[29] While these findings suggest that shareholders of firms with boards dominated by outsiders fare better in takeovers than those of firms with boards dominated by insiders, there is no convincing evidence that greater board independence (as measured by proportion of insiders to outsiders) correlates with greater firm profitability or faster growth.[30] Further, from 1985 to 1995, low-profitability firms increased the proportion of outsiders on the board; but an increase in the proportion of non-affiliated directors on their boards was not accompanied by improved profitability.[31] More

---

26  See Chun I. Lee, Stuart Rosenstein, Nanda Rangan and Wallace N. Davidson III, 'Board Composition and Shareholder Wealth: The Case of Management Buyouts', *Financial Management* (Spring 1992), 58, 65–8.

27  See John W. Byrd and Kent A. Hickman, 'Do Outside Directors Monitor Managers? Evidence from Tender Offer Bids', *Journal of Financial Economics* (1992), 195, 203–4, 207.

28  See Paul Mallette and Karen Fowler, 'Effects of Board Composition and Stock Ownership on the Adoption of "Poison Pills"', *Academy of Management Journal*, 35 (1992), 1010, 1023; Sunil Wahal, Kenneth W. Wiles and Marc Zenner, 'Who Opts Out of State Antitakover Protection? The Case of Pennsylvania's SB 1310', *Financial Management*, 24(3) (Autumn 1995), 22, 26–7; Chamu Sundaramurthy, Paula Rechner and Weiren Wang, 'Governance Antecedents of Board Entrenchment: The Case of Classified Board Provisions', *Journal of Management*, 22 (1996), 783.

29  See James A. Brickley, Jeffery L. Coles and Rory L. Terry, 'Outside Directors and the Adoption of Poison Pills', *Journal of Financial Economics*, 35 (1994), 371.

30  See Sanjai Bhagat and Bernard Black, 'The Uncertain Relationship Between Board Composition and Firm Performance', *Business Lawyer*, 54 (1999), 921–63.

31  See Sanjai Bhagat and Bernard Black, 'Board Independence and Long Term Firm Performance', working paper available via http://papers.ssrn.com (February 2000).

generally, changes in board composition do not necessarily produce significant changes in firm performance over time, given no significant correlation between board composition and various measures of firm performance.[32]

Attempts to link specific board governance to corporate performance have thus produced inconclusive results.[33] Numerous analytical studies have been based on a methodology that links one or very few elements

---

32  See Barry D. Baysinger and Henry N. Butler, 'Corporate Governance and the Boards of Directors: Performance Effects of Changes in Board Composition', *Journal of Law, Economics and Organization*, 1 (1985), 101, 116; Benjamin E. Hermalin and Michael S. Weisbach, 'The Effects of Board Composition and Direct Incentives on Firm Performance', *Financial Management*, 20 (Winter 1991), 111; Paul W. MacAvoy, Scott Cantor, Jim Dana and Sarah Peck, 'ALI Proposals for Increased Control of the Corporation by the Board of Directors: An Economic Analysis', in *Statement of the Business Roundtable on the American Law Institute's Proposed 'Principles of Corporate Governance and Structure: Restatement and Recommendations'* (1983), C-1, C-34; Hamid Mehran, 'Executive Compensation Structure, Ownership and Firm Performance', *Journal of Financial Economics*, 38 (1995), 163.

33  See, e.g., Barry D. Baysinger and Henry N. Butler, 'Revolution Versus Evolution in Corporation Law: The ALI's Project and the Independent Director', *George Washington Law Review*, 52 (1984), 557, 562–6 (concluding that 'as corporate board independence increases, corporate financial performance tends to increase'); James A. Brickley, J.L. Coles and R.L. Terry, 'Outside Directors and the Adoption of Poison Pills', *Journal of Financial Economics*, 35 (1994), 371, 371–2 (examining the stock price effects of poison pills to measure the extent to which more outside directors further promote shareholder interests); Victor Brudney, 'The Independent Director – Heavenly City or Potemkin Village?', *Harvard Law Review*, 95 (1982), 597, 601–2 (analysing the obstacles independent directors have encountered in policing managerial conflicts of interest and in monitoring the maximization of shareholder wealth); John W. Byrd and Kent A. Hickman, 'Do Outside Directors Monitor Managers? Evidence from Tender Offer Bids', *Journal of Financial Economics*, 32 (1992), 195, 196; Rajeswararao S. Chaganti, S. Sharma and V. Mahajan, 'Corporate Board Size, Composition and Corporate Failures in Retailing Industry', *Journal of Management Studies*, 22 (1985), 400, 406–7 ('Corporate performance measured in terms of return on investment, stock appreciation, or relative standing of the firm in its industry, may be associated more with technical expertise and managerial experience of inside directors than any other attribute of the boardroom'); Benjamin E. Hermalin and Michael S. Weisbach, 'The Effects of Board Composition and Direct Incentives on Firm Performance', *Financial Management*, 20 (1991), 101, 101–12 (concluding that 'if such a relationship does exist, it is small with little economic significance'); Anil Shivdasani, 'Board Composition, Ownership Structure, and Hostile Takeovers', *Journal of Accounting and Economics*, 16 (1993), 167, 167–9 (limited impact of board and ownership structure on the likelihood of a hostile takeover).

of board structure to measures of corporate performance, such as stock price, or to a single corporate event, such as a CEO firing. The early studies found that the percentage of non-management directors on a board correlated positively with frequency of CEO replacement,[34] and positive response to takeover bids.[35] However, when examined with other factors included, it became difficult to establish such relationships.[36] Our position is that no set of structural characteristics of a board can be expected to correlate with better corporate performance without

---

34 See generally Michael S. Weisbach, 'Outside Directors and CEO Turnover', *Journal of Financial Economics*, 20 (1988), 431 (CEO turnover was more sensitive to firm performance in firms with a higher proportion of outside directors; boards with at least 60 per cent independent directors were more likely than other boards to fire a poorly performing CEO; but CEO termination rate for firms was only 1.3 per cent higher for those with 60 per cent independent boards than for those with 40 per cent or fewer independent directors; and, for firms with above average stock price performance, CEO turnover was lower for firms with 60 per cent independent boards).

35 See generally Byrd and Hickman, 'Outside Directors', 195–221 (tender offer bidders with majority-independent boards offer lower takeover premia and experience zero stock price change on average; bidders without such boards suffer stock price losses during takeovers of 1.8 per cent on average); James F. Cotter, A. Shivdasani and M. Zenner, 'Do Independent Directors Enhance Target Shareholder Wealth During Tender Offers?', *Journal of Financial Economics*, 43 (1997), 195, 204–5 (tender offer targets having majority-independent boards realized roughly 20 per cent higher stock price returns between 1989 and 1992 than targets without majority-independent boards; the initial tender offer premium, the bid premium revision, and the target shareholder gains over the tender offer period were higher; it appears that such independent boards were more likely to use resistance strategies to enhance shareholder wealth); cf. Shivdasani, 'Board Composition', 167–98 (companies with 'high-quality' directors, as defined by the number of boards on which they serve – apparently the more the better – are less likely to become takeover targets).

36 The link between board characteristics and company performance is difficult, if not impossible, to isolate because of the multitude of other factors that impact corporate performance more directly. See, e.g., Robert Gertner and Steven N. Kaplan, *The Value Maximizing Board* (University of Chicago and National Bureau of Economic Research Working Paper 1996), 2 (indicating that 'the link between board structure and performance occurs concurrently with numerous other factors', thereby contributing to a 'noise' problem with performance regressions including board characteristics as independent variables). Moreover, boards are prone to restructure themselves in times of poor corporate performance, and therefore board structure is partially determined by past corporate performance. See Hermalin and Weisbach, 'Effects of Board Composition', 88, 102 (using panel data and instrumental variables to control for changes in board compositions due to past performance).

further analysis of its implications for board conduct. Ambivalent results from empirical studies on the link between structural aspects of governance and corporate performance do not however disprove a link between board conduct and investor returns. Even in the face of ambiguous studies, we have to begin with Darwin's logic that the independent and professional board is the 'grain in the balance' of survival in the long run, so that positive effects on performance have to follow.[37]

But we further note that the strategic, managerial, and organizational determinants of corporate performance are complex and interrelated. Merger or acquisition activity may cancel other determinants, such as board activism. An unexpected turn of the business cycle, or changes in product demand, can reverse the performance rating of a corporation in less than a year. Additionally, from outside the corporation looking in, it is difficult to determine whether active boards have actually been making decisions that could improve managerial performance. Given these complications, it is understandable that previous attempts to determine whether board activism improved performance were inconclusive.

---

37  We note in passing that the search for econometric proof that good governance by an active and independent board matters to corporate performance by some has not seemed all that important. As the Nobel laureate in economics, Robert M. Solow, writes, 'in economics, model-builders busywork is to refine their ideas to ask questions to which the available data cannot give the answer ... We have the overeducated in pursuit of the unknowable.' See Robert M. Solow, 'How Did Economics Get That Way and What Way Did It Get?', *Journal of American Academy of Arts and Sciences* (Winter 1997), 57. Solow also noted, 'there is a tendency to undervalue keen observation and shrewd generalization.... There is a lot to be said in favor of staring at the piece of reality you are studying and asking, just what is going on here?' (ibid., 56). But 'does the absence of conclusive empirical proof ... mean we should ignore the obvious linkage?' See Ira M. Millstein, 'The State of Corporate Governance', Speech Before the National Association of Corporate Directors, 1 November 1993, in Robert A.G. Monks and Nell Minow, *Corporate Governance* (1995), 445, 451. The argument is as follows:

> 'To me it is intuitively correct that to maximize the corporation's wealth-producing capacity we must ensure that the accountability mechanism provided in the legal structure of the governance system works ...' Think about it: no one questions that the CEO's performance matters a great deal to corporate performance. And the board is charged with hiring the best CEO it can find, helping the CEO set goals and priorities for the long-term viability of the corporation, monitoring his or her accomplishments against those goals and, if necessary, replacing him or her in a timely manner. How can board performance not matter to corporate performance?

But who would assert that corporations would be equally or better situated if governed once again by management, with oversight from a rubber-stamp board? An active and independent board of directors working for shareholders would seem to benefit the corporation by reducing the losses which are inherent in the separation of ownership from control fundamental to the modern corporation.

Encouraged by this logic and not discouraged by the inconclusiveness of previous econometric studies, we develop a different approach to defining governance conduct and to measuring performance. In Chapter 5 we present a study which moves beyond efforts to correlate board structure with stock returns in order to link behaviour in the governance process with the earnings generated from operations.

# 5
# A New Approach for Determining the Effect of Strong Governance on Corporate Performance

*Paul W. MacAvoy*

In 1997, we conducted a study of 154 US companies in which we found a positive correlation between US corporations with active and independent boards of directors and Economic Value Added (EVA™).[1] This study has since then been noted as one of the few to look at board independence from a behavioural rather than structural perspective.'[2]

In that study and in this further work, of the same kind, we choose to use a methodology based on the logical foundations that led Darwin to his conclusions.[3] We have observed that certain changes in board

1 See Ira M. Millstein and Paul W. MacAvoy, 'The Active Board of Directors and Performance of the Large Publicly Traded Corporation', *Columbia Law Review*, 98 (June 1998) (data analysis 1991–95, showing that US corporations with active and independent boards of directors generated higher economic profit supports the 'reasonable assumption' that corporate governance matters to corporate performance).
2 Bradley A. Helms with Richard Koppes, 'Statistical Alchemy: How Methodological Shortcomings in the Inquiries into the Financial Impact of Corporate Governance Reform Prevent the Wall Streets of the World From Reaching a Consensus About the Value of Good Corporate Governance', *Business Law International* (2000), 218.
3 See Charles Darwin, *On the Origin of Species by Means of Natural Selection* (1859), 467, quoted in Daniel C. Dennett, *Darwin's Dangerous Idea* (1995), 41. 'More individuals are born than can possibly survive. A grain in the balance will determine which individual shall live and which shall die – which variety or species shall increase in number, and which shall decrease; or finally become extinct.'

practice brought activism to the boardrooms of some large corporations that focused on processes that monitored and incentivized management to deliver on strategies that enhance returns to shareholders. Although the only certain way to know whether that takes place is to be present in the boardroom, we can hypothesize that certain elements of board process indicate that such activism is present: that is, the presence of such process, not structure, can be used to identify reform governance.

We take the step of identifying those boards that embrace a culture of professionalism distinct from management and that have asserted control over processes to monitor and control management.[4] We test our hypothesis that the existence of those boards can be associated with better management and this corporate performance where performance is measured by economic value added (i.e. operating earnings in excess of the costs of capital). Well-governed corporations versus those that do not appear to follow the activist practices and procedures should generate higher economic value added.

We examine 128 large publicly traded US corporations and determine, based on criteria outlined below, whether the board in each case is active or inactive in the governance process. This sample was created by utilizing the same information we relied on in our earlier study: the responses received by the California Public Employees Retirement System (CalPERS), and CalPERS grading of these responses, to letters it sent to 300 of its portfolio companies asking whether they had board guidelines along the lines of the guidelines adopted by the GM board.[5]

---

4 See NACD, *Report on the NACD Blue Ribbon Commission of Director Professionalism* (1996), 3–6.

5 For the initial cross-sectional data analysis, we used the geometric mean, which de-emphasizes the effect of year-to-year variation upon the rate of return, instead of the arithmetic mean, which does not. The sample consisted of the 300 largest domestic equity holdings in the CalPERS portfolio, exclusive of General Motors (which was the promulgator of the standards). See CalPERS, 'Responses, Final Report: Company Responses to Request for Board Governance Self-Evaluation' (1995), 1 (on file with the authors); CalPERS Press Release, 'CalPERS Announces Results of Governance Survey', 31 May 1995 (on file with the authors). Jostens, Inc., which voluntarily joined the survey, and Lockheed Martin, which resulted from the merger of two companies already in the survey, were added. In the database, Lockheed Martin data for 1994–1995 were used to extend Lockheed data for the period after the merger, according to COMPUSTAT™.

We began with this list of 300 firms as we compiled our sample, and found that two firms were undergoing restructuring and 76 firms failed to respond to CalPERS. The remaining 222 firms became the first sample group for the study. We then used the COMPUSTAT™ database to retrieve financial performance data that allowed us to generate earnings estimates for 1991–2001. We believe this time period, consisting of three years prior to the CalPERS study and eight years afterwards, is sufficient to calculate long-run values for returns and average costs of capital while accounting for year-to-year changes in industry and general economic conditions. After taking various factors into account, which we describe in more detail later in the chapter, the final sample consisted of 128 companies. A full description of how the final sample was derived can be found in Appendix A, and a complete listing of the firms and their returns for this period is found in Appendix B.

## Metrics for board independence and professionalism

We have not been able to observe and record whether specific boards were participating directly in strategic planning, and the motivating and monitoring of management performance. The doors to boardrooms of 128 companies were not open to us. However, based on our experience with numerous boards as members or advisers, we believe that acceptable surrogates for indicating the presence of professional boards include:

- the presence of independent board leadership, through a non-executive chair or a lead director, able to act without relying solely on initiatives from management;
- directors meeting periodically without management to provide the opportunity to evaluate management against the plan for corporate performance;
- the establishment of rules or guidelines establishing an independent relationship between the board and management as to how to conduct the business of the corporation.

When one of these indicators is present, by our logic we assume that the board is independent, and hence is the 'grain in the balance' in favour of exerting pressure on management to achieve maximum financial performance. In our opinion, these indicia identify companies that have independent boards that practice 'professionalism' and in that sense are well governed. We concede that this is a judgment on our part, but it is one based on a host of personal observations and extensive experience with boards both with and without these practices.

As this time, boards are not required to disclose extensive information about how they operate and therefore documentation, even as to these indicia set forth, is limited.[6] However, the responses that CalPERS generated by asking companies to review the GM guidelines contain relevant information for determining their presence. Despite the fact that the responses were not in any standardized form, indicia of 'professionalism' could be inferred from the letter responses. We herein rely on the analysis of those responses from our earlier study to determine whether a professional board was present. If a company represented in its letter to CalPERS that it had an independent board, as we have

---

6 Note that listing rule amendments proposed in the summer of 2002 by the NYSE and NASDAQ will require greater disclosure. For example, if the SEC approves the proposals as they stand now, NYSE boards will be required to convene regular 'executive' sessions of independent directors outside the presence of management; adopt and disclose corporate governance guidelines and charters for compensation and nominating/governance committees (audit committee charter disclosure is already required); and adopt and disclose a code of business conduct and ethics applicable to directors and officers. The corporate governance guidelines would have to address director compensation, responsibilities, qualification standards, and orientation and continuing education, as well as management succession and board performance. Although many companies have taken steps to implement these rules, the new standards have not, as of this writing, been approved. See 'Corporate Governance Rule Proposals Reflecting Recommendations from the NYSE Corporate Accountability and Listing Standards Committee' (16 August 2002) available at http://www. nyse.com/pdfs/corp_gov_pro_b.pdf; NASDAQ, 'Affected Marketplace Rules: 4200(a)(14), 4200(a)(15), 4350(c), 4350(d), and IM-4350-4' (9 October 2002) available at http://www.nasdaq.com/about/2002_141.pdf; cf. Constance E. Bagley and Richard H. Koppes, 'Leader of the Pack: A Proposal for Disclosure of Board Leadership Structure', *San Diego Law Review*, 34 (1997), 149, 152 (recommending that the New York Stock Exchange and the National Association of Securities Dealers amend their listing policies to require listed companies to disclose in proxy statements whether the company has a separate independent chairman and, if not, whether the board has designated an independent director to function as a leader of the board's independent directors).

defined, or that it followed 'substantially all' of the GM guidelines, then we conclude that professional board governance could be associated with that company; but we note that this evaluation is based on how each company chose to report to CalPERS. We did not conduct interviews, and neither did we attempt to substitute any knowledge of the company that we may independently have possessed as to the professionalism of its board.

As in our earlier study, once a professional board has been identified by adherence to a certain letter response, we stipulate that good governance is present at that corporation and that such a corporation is likely to exhibit superior economic performance. To test this relationship, we use the governance letter grades assigned to companies by CalPERS during its survey. We identify corporations as well governed if the CalPERS grade was A+; taking steps to become well governed if the grades were A or B; and, poorly governed if the grades given were C, D or F.

## Metrics for performance

Analysts of corporate performance use a variety of measures to evaluate results, based on criteria that range across productive or allocative efficiency, technological progress, employment, even qualitative fairness measures.[7] Measures that are central to fulfilling goals for investors, or to enhancing company access to capital, centre on either internal corporate earnings or stock market returns to investors. Measures of internal returns include earnings or net income per share, predicted future earnings or net income and, in various guises, economic value added to capital invested. While each of these measures yields valuable information, we focus on economic value added which is the excess earnings to capital invested, over and above the competitive required returns (the cost of capital) as estimated from the corporation's annual income statements.

We did not choose to use a stock market-based measure of performance, such as annual stock price change plus dividends. After shareholders

---

7 See F.M. Scherer and David Ross, *Industrial Market Structure and Economic Performance* (3rd edn, 1990) 4–5. For the performance criteria of 'workable competition', see p. 54.

have capitalized the expected gains from putting in a professional board, in the year it takes place, annual gains for companies that are well governed should be the same as for companies that are not.[8] We chose a form of economic value added, EVA™ because it provides a metric for a company's ability to 'generate economic profits and, thereby, create wealth directly for shareholders'.[9] This is the earnings after interest, taxes, and depreciation, of the net income: that is, the '"residual"... after the cost of capital has been subtracted'.[10] A positive value for excess return indicates that a company is adding value to the wealth of shareholders and a negative value indicates that it is destroying value.[11]

As an indicator of corporate performance, this metric offers a number of advantages. Proponents of EVA™, of which we develop a variant, believe the following to be true.

---

8 See, e.g., Alfred Rappaport, *Creating Shareholder Value: The New Standard for Business Performance* (1986), 19–49 (discussion of earnings per share, return on investment, and return on equity as performance measures); Alfred Jackson, 'The How and Why of EVA™ at CS First Boston', *Journal of Applied Corporate Finance* (Spring 1996), 98, 99–101 (discussion of earnings per share and EVA™); The Fourth Mitsui Life Symposium on Global Financial Markets, 'EVA™ and Shareholder Value in Japan', *Journal of Applied Corporate Finance* (Winter 1997), 102–3 (Joel Stern discussing return on equity and EVA™); Symposium, 'Stern Stewart EVA™ Roundtable', *Journal of Applied Corporate Finance* (Summer 1994), 46, 46–70 (hereinafter 'Stern Stewart Roundtable') (discussing EVA™ in relation to more conventional measures of corporate performance such as Earnings Per Share and Return On Equity); 'Valuing Companies: A Star to Sail By?', *The Economist*, 2 August 1997, 53, 53–5 (comparing EVA™, 'cash flow return on investment,' and other performance metrics). Economic Value Added™ and EVA™ are registered trademarks of Stern Stewart & Co.

9 Laura Walbert, 'The 1994 Stern Stewart Performance 1000', *Journal of Applied Corporate Finance* (Winter 1995), 105 (discussing EVA™). For a discussion of shareholder value creation, see Rappaport, *Creating Shareholder Value*, 65–77.

10 See 'Stern Stewart Roundtable', 49 (discussing EVA™). Roberto Goizueta, former CEO of Coca-Cola, is quoted as having told *Fortune*: 'You only get richer if you invest money at a higher return than the cost of that money to you. Everybody knows that – but many seem to forget it.' See Irwin Ross, 'The 1996 Stern Stewart Performance 1000', *Journal of Applied Corporate Finance* (Winter 1997), 116.

11 See 'Stern Stewart Roundable', 49 (discussing EVA™); Walbert, 'The 1994 Stern Stewart Performance 1000', 106 (discussing EVA™).

1   It relies on the assumption that 'the prime financial objective of any company ought to be to maximize the wealth of the shareholders'.[12]

2   It is straightforward, using one earnings measure that can be applied to all corporations,[13] thereby reducing the need to rely on multiple, and sometimes conflicting measures.[14]

3   It can be utilized for a business, 'at different stages of growth . . . whether a business is capital-intensive or a service business'.[15]

---

12  G. Bennett Stewart III, 'EVA™: Fact and Fantasy', *Journal of Applied Corporate Finance* (Summer 1994), 71, 72. Stewart states:

> Basic corporate finance and microeconomic theory tells us that the prime financial objective of any firm ought to be maximize the wealth of its shareholders. This objective not only serves the interests of the firm's owners; it is also the rule that ensures that scarce resources of all kinds are allocated, managed, and redeployed as efficiently as possible – which in turn maximizes the wealth of society at large. (ibid., 72)

See also, e.g., NACD, *Report on Director Professionalism*, 1 ('The objective of the corporation (and therefore of its management and board of directors) is to conduct its business activities so as to enhance corporate profit and shareholder gain.').

13  See Stewart, 'EVA™', 77. Although EVA™ is 'simple' in that it is one concept with broad applications, Stewart's advisory company, Stern Stewart & Co., recommends that individual companies adopt 'highly customized' EVA™ definitions. Stewart states:

> In defining and refining its EVA™ measure, Stern Stewart has identified a total of 164 performance measurement issues, including methods of addressing shortcomings in conventional GAAP [generally accepted accounting principles] accounting. . . . For most of these accounting issues, we have . . . devised a variety of practical methods to modify reported accounting results in order to improve the accuracy with which EVA™ measures real economic income. (ibid., 73)

Stewart states that in practice Stern Stewart addresses 20–25 necessary key issues for an individual company in detail and recommends 5–10 adjustments: see ibid., 73–4. Our implementation of returns in excess of the cost of capital differs from the EVA™ metric by relying solely on raw generally accepted accounting practice (GAAP) data, given that we cannot make such adjustments. We cannot evaluate the differences this creates in estimates, but rather rely on the methodology and the known quality of GAAP published data.

14  See 'Stern Stewart Roundtable', 52.

15  Walbert, '1994 Stern Stewart Performance 1000', 106 (quoting Bennett Stewart).

4 It 'takes into account the amount...of corporate investment and... specifies a...required rate of return that must be earned on capital employed' to cover the opportunity cost of this investment.[16]

5 It 'explicitly acknowledges a cost of equity capital' which 'is [determined by] shareholder value'.[17]

But this measure of corporate performance is subject to limitations. Because it is retrospective, being based on calculation of the residual from historical operating revenues and operating costs, it can differ significantly from current stock market measures of shareholder returns (a measure of value with which investors are more familiar).[18] However, as we have argued, the forward-looking alternative measure, the stock price, is not a good measure for the purpose of evaluating relative performance of some corporations versus other corporations because the governance factors are capitalized in the stock price once, rather than determining year-to-year change in value to shareholders. Estimating this over-time increased capitalized value is exceedingly difficult.[19] Financial logic holds that a stock price is equal to the

---

16 'Stern Stewart Roundtable', 49 (quoting Joel Stern).

17 Timothy J. Sheehan, 'To EVA™ or Not to EVA™: Is That the Question?', *Journal of Applied Corporate Finance* (Summer 1994), 85.

18 See Ross, '1996 Stern Stewart Performance 1000', 116. In discussing market value added and EVA™, Ross states, 'While EVA™ measures current performance, share prices reflect expectations; good current EVA™ numbers must hold forth the promise of future EVA™ improvement for the market to react favorably': ibid.; see also Jeffrey M. Bacidore *et al.*, 'The Search for the Best Financial Performance Measure', *Financial Analysts Journal*, 53 (May–June 1997), 11. ('The obvious metric for judging firm performance is the stock price itself...Stock price, however (or returns based on stock price), may not be an efficient contracting parameter because it is driven by many factors beyond the control of the firm's executives.')

19 See Thomas E. Copeland and J. Fred Weston, *Financial Theory and Corporate Policy* (3rd edn, 1988), 38 ('Shareholders' wealth...is the present value of their stream of residual cash flows, discounted at the cost of equity capital'); William F. Sharpe *et al.*, *Investments* (6th edn, 1998), 568–9 (describing the 'capitalization of income method of valuation'): The 'true' or 'intrinsic' value of any asset is based on the cash flows that the investor expects to receive in the future from owning the asset. Because these cash flows are expected in the future, they are adjusted by a discount rate to reflect not only the time value of money but also the riskiness of the cash flows (ibid.).

discounted present value of future excess earnings. To calculate this governance-specific increase in present value, and thus the value of better governance, requires determination of when investors learned that company performance would be affected in the future by a change currently taking in governance.[20] Thus, while our valuation measure is limited because it is historically based, it does not reflect speculative expectations of future effects as would some measure based on share price.

At a more practical level, it is well known that EVA™ estimates explain less than half of the variance in share value from company to company; the rest is random, or dependent on widely diverse shareholder assessments of future prospects.[21] But it measures what the company has actually accomplished in the 1990s and early 2000s, rather than what investors predict that management (and board) will do in the future. An EVA™ estimate provides a measure relatively free from factors that affect stock price but which are outside the company's control, such as changes in general stock market returns and interest rates. We believe that managerial performance, and that of the board of directors, is better measured by value added in income statements than by share price change.

---

20 See, e.g., Rappaport, *Creating Shareholder Value*, 51–5 (estimating future cash flows from operations and operating profit margins). In estimating an appropriate discount rate, it is important to emphasize that the relative weights attached to debt and equity, respectively, are neither predicated on dollars the firm has raised in the past, nor do they constitute the relative proportions of dollars the firm plans to raise in the current year. Instead, the relevant weights should be based on the proportions of debt and equity that the firm targets for its capital structure over the long-term planning period. Ibid., 56; see also Sharpe *et al.*, *Investments*, 568–9; Stephen F. O'Byrne, 'EVA™ and Market Value', *Journal of Applied Corporate Finance* (Spring 1996), 118 ('Part of a company's current market value – and hence its multiple of earnings and capital – reflects its prospects for profitable growth in the future').

21 Cf. Rawley Thomas, The Boston Consulting Group, *Economic Value Added (EVA) Versus Cash Value Added (CVA): Stern Stewart Versus BCG/HOLT: Empirical Comparisons* (22 May 1993), 8 (on file with the authors) (chart entitled 'Correlations of Market Value Added Versus Stern Stewart's EVA and Holt's CVA' indicates that the $R^2$ (per cent of explained variance) of stock price variation explained by variation in EVA never exceeded 0.33 in any year from 1982 to 1991 and was 0.09 in 1986).

Even so, this measure is hampered by the difficulties of estimating the cost of capital,[22] especially in companies that have multiple business units[23] with joint costs or revenue.[24] However, these limitations exist for any measure that estimates capital costs in an attempt to measure performance.[25]

Finally, using an excess return measure relies on the assumption that the corporate goal is to add to earnings in excess of the costs of capital as we have indicated in the proceeding chapters, this is not always the case although we believe it should be. Sheehan has noted, 'Others

---

22 See, e.g., Rappaport, *Creating Shareholder Value*, 174–81 (selecting performance measures and criteria in evaluating and compensating executives). Rappaport states that proper criteria should be valid, verifiable, controllable ('if a performance measure is used to assess an executive, he or she should have a reasonable degree of control over the results being measured'), global, and communicable: ibid., 175–6; see also Bacidore *et al.*, 'The Search' (discussing EVA™ and proposing REVA (refined economic value added) as performance measures). ('Any financial performance measure used in managerial compensation, on the one hand, must be correlated highly with changes in shareholder wealth and, on the other, should not be subject to all of the randomness and 'noise' inherent in a firm's stock price.')

23 Cf. 'Stern Stewart Roundtable', 63 (statements of S. Abraham Ravid and Jerold Zimmerman).

24 See ibid., 68.

25 See ibid. Ravid states:

EVA™ has the same problems that we have always had with discounted cash flow. For one thing, a precise estimate of the cost of capital is very difficult to achieve especially in decentralized companies with many different business units. Also, estimating expected future cash flows is more of an art than a science. Because you are investing today and hoping that something will happen a few years hence, there is a great deal of uncertainty about those estimates. You cannot escape this imprecision, whether you use EVA™ or discounted cash flow. (ibid., 63)

Zimmerman states:

That's ultimately the conundrum that you have with EVA™ or any other performance measure. You can allocate costs down to the penny, and they will be right in an arithmetic sense. But they do not tell you anything about the real economic profitability of producing that joint product. Neither EVA™ nor any accounting system is set up to handle this kind of problem that arises from synergies. (ibid., 68)

have proposed that shareholders are only one constituency and that the long-term success (and survival) of the company depends on benefits received by a broader set of constituencies including customers, employees, and suppliers of labor, technology, and capital.'[26] We bypass that search for appropriate 'benefits received', principally because that position was widely employed as the rationale for the stagnation and loss of competitive position of some of the largest corporations during the 1970s and 1980s. We make the assumption that residual earnings maximization is the goal that good governance seeks to make management achieve.

## Methodology

Our method of calculating excess returns, adapted from EVA™, is to subtract a 'company's cost of capital, which includes the costs of both equity and debt, from its net operating profits after tax'.[27] This method generates dollar estimates of excess returns. For example, if Company A earns $100 million after taxes and interest and has a cost of equity capital equal to $70 million, its excess return would be $30 million. It is difficult to make meaningful comparisons between companies and across industries using individual company dollar estimates, however. The larger company in many instances becomes identified as the better performer, even though its ability to generate a larger dollar return may be a function of its size rather than of managerial acumen. Consequently, this study measures the rate of return on invested capital (ROIC) minus the weighted average cost of capital (WACC).[28] The difference represents the percentage rate of excess net income that cumulates as wealth for investors.

By constructing an estimate of the total value of capital (operating invested capital, OIC) in the company (outstanding value of debt and preferred equity plus stock market value of common equity), the

---

26 Sheehan, 'To EVA™ or Not to EVA™', 86. But see Rappaport, *Creating Share-holder Value*, 1 ('The principle that the fundamental objective of the business corporation is to increase the value of its shareholders' investment is widely accepted').

27 Walbert, '1994 Stern Stewart Performance 1000', 106 (discussing EVA™).

28 See text below and accompanying notes below.

percentage return on invested capital ROIC is estimated by dividing
operating profit by the value of capital,[29] such that:

$$\text{ROIC} = \frac{\text{NOPLAT}}{\text{Operating Invested Capital}}$$

NOPLAT is net operating profit less adjusted taxes, or more commonly
EBIT less adjusted taxes.[30] The percentage weighted average cost of
capital[31] is estimated by dividing financing costs by the total amount of
book value of debt, preferred stock and common stock, such that:

$$\text{WACC} = \frac{\text{Interest Cost of Debt + Dividend Cost of Preferred Stock + Cost of Common Stock}}{\text{Debt + Preferred Stock + Common Stock}}$$

To calculate the denominator of WACC, we utilized figures from
COMPUSTAT™ [32] for the total amount of debt, preferred shares, and
common stock. To determine the numerator of WACC, we calculated
(i) the cost of debt, which equalled interest expense (less the tax shield

---

29  The denominator of ROIC calculation, Operating Invested Capital (OIC),
is defined as follows: OIC = Operating Working Capital + Net Plant, Property
and Equipment + Other Assets – Other Liabilities + Goodwill. Goodwill, the
value that is assigned to acquired assets to represent the amount paid over
the book value of those assets, is an intangible asset that is calculated
retrospectively, and is of questionable utility in this study. The results listed
in this study do not incorporate the effects of goodwill on the capital
stock. Operating Working Capital (OWC), in turn, is defined as follows:
OWC = Operating Cash + Excess Marketable Securities + Accounts Receivable
+ Inventories + Other Current Assets (Less Excess Marketable Securities) –
Accounts Payable – Other Current Liabilities.

30  NOPLAT = EBIT – Taxes on EBIT – Change in Deferred Taxes. EBIT, earnings
before income taxes, represents the pretax 'bottom line' of earnings on
operations, and consists of: Net Sales – Cost of Goods Sold – Selling, General,
and Administrative Expenses – Depreciation [+ Other Operating Expense/Income
+ Adjustment for Operating Leases + Adjustment for Retirement-Related
Liabilities].

31  For a discussion of WACC, see Copeland and Weston, *Financial Theory*, 39,
444–51; Tom Copeland, Tim Koller and Jack Murin, *Valuation: Measuring and
Managing the Value of Companies* (2nd edn 1995), 239–73. The equation on
page 240 of *Valuation* is summarized in that shown above. For the WACC
calculations utilized in this study, see Appendix A.

32  COMPUSTAT™ is a registered trademark of the McGraw-Hill Companies.

effect of interest deductibility);[33] (ii) the cost of preferred stock, which equalled dividends paid to preferred shareholders;[34] and (iii) the cost of common stock, which equalled the opportunity cost to investors of holding the stock[35] (i.e., the 'rate that the firm must earn to entice an investor to invest in [its] equity').[36]

The cost of a company's equity is estimated from stock market data and consists of the sum of '(i) a risk-free rate of return, (ii) the premium for average risk over the risk-free rate, times (iii) the premium for covariance of the [company's] equity relative to the average risk stocks'.[37] The percentage cost of equity is defined as:

---

33 The cost of debt is defined as $r^*\ (1-t)$, where $r$ is interest paid and $t$ is a marginal corporate tax rate. Because interest payments are tax-deductible by the company, the interest cost is reduced by the value of the deduction. See Copeland and Weston, *Financial Theory*, 39; Rappaport, *Creating Shareholder Value*, 56 ('Since interest on debt is tax deductible, the rate of return that must be earned on debt-financed instruments is the after-tax cost of debt'). This study uses marginal tax rates because the companies in the study are sufficiently large that the difference between marginal and average tax rates is assumed to be negligible. For the cost of debt figures utilized in this study, see Appendix A.

34 See Copeland and Weston, *Financial Theory*, 480 ('The before- and after-tax costs are the same for preferred stock because preferred dividends are not deductible as an expense before taxes.'); see also Appendix A (cost of preferred stock figures utilized in this study).

35 'The required rate of return is the opportunity cost to the investor of investing scarce resources elsewhere in opportunities with equivalent risk': Copeland and Weston, *Financial Theory*, 437 (discussing debt and equity investment funds). 'Shareholders will require the rate of return on new projects to be greater than the opportunity cost of the funds supplied by them and the bondholders. This condition is equivalent to requiring that original shareholders' wealth increase' (ibid., 444–5) (discussing WACC); see Appendix A (cost of common stock figures utilized in this study).

36 Peter V. Pantaleo and Barry W. Ridings, 'Reorganization Value', *Business Lawyer*, 51 (1996), 419, 433 (discussing valuation fundamentals for Chapter 11 reorganization valuations); see also, e.g., Rappaport, *Creating Shareholder Value*, 57 ('There is some implicit rate of return required to attract investors to purchase the firm's stock and to induce shareholders to hold their shares. This rate is the relevant cost of equity capital').

37 Pantaleo and Ridings, 'Reorganization Value', 433; see also Rappaport, *Creating Shareholder Value*, 57–9 (indicating that cost of equity can be estimated as the sum of the risk-free rate and an equity risk premium, which in turn can be computed as the product of the market risk premium for equity and the individual stock's systematic risk).

$$\text{Equity Cost} = \text{beta}(R_M - R_F) + R_F {}^{38}$$

$R_M$ is the rate of return on the index portfolio of stock market shares (i.e., the average rate), $R_F$ is the risk-free rate, and beta represents the adjustment for covariance of the stock's price with the market index net of the risk-free rate. As Pantaleo and Ridings explain:

> This formula, in essence, provides that a firm's cost of equity is equal to the sum of the risk-free rate of return plus a risk premium (i.e., a return above the risk-free rate). The risk premium for the firm is calculated by multiplying the risk premium that the equity market generally must pay to attract investors by the firm's 'beta' which . . . reflects the risk associated with an equity investment in the firm relative to [that] of an investment in the equity market as a whole.[39]

The three component percentages of cost of capital are weighted according to the relative proportion that each represents in the company's capital structure. The resulting percentage cost of capital is the WACC to be subtracted from the rate of return ROIC to provide an index of excess return that captures a variety of effects, including the tax shield effects of debt, the market sensitivity of equity, and the cost effects of debt–equity ratio decisions of management.

## Estimation and analysis of the governance/corporate performance relationship

Given that board performance is not the sole determinant of economic performance, we seek to identify the effects of other determinants and attempt to control for them. Two of the more important candidates are the economic performance of a firm's industry and the life-cycle position

---

38  This equation for the rate is based on the Capital Asset Pricing Model (CAPM). CAPM is based on the premise that equity cost can be derived implicitly from the financial markets in which the equity must compete. Under CAPM, the price of the equity is modelled as a linear function of the difference between market return and the rate of return on risk-free assets. For a discussion of CAPM, see Copeland and Weston, *Financial Theory*, 193–219; Sharpe *et al.*, *Investments*, 261–77. For a discussion of calculating the cost of capital, see Rappaport, *Creating Shareholder Value*, 55–9. For an explanation of the measures of market rate, risk-free rate, and beta utilized in this study, see Appendix A.

39  Pantaleo and Ridings, 'Reorganization Value', 433–4.

of the firm within that industry. Industry performance matters because some firms are in industries that experience substantial demand growth, while others are in industries that are stagnant, or that faced decline in the 1990s and early 2000s. For example, a company in the aluminium industry, which supplies a mature, commoditized product, is likely to be less profitable than a company employing the same good governance practices in the pharmaceutical industry, which features highly differentiated products, significant new product development, and substantial annual increases in demand for these new products.

Another factor in performance is the regulatory environment in which companies operate. While virtually all industries encounter some form of regulation, the effects on profitability are particularly great in electric power and telecommunications, where companies must cope with regulatory regimes that limit the rate of return to costs of capital, to prevent the long-term realization of any economic value added. Under such regimes, management has a reduced incentive to try to generate value added, since such gains are likely to be allocated to consumers in reduced prices rather than to investors in increased returns.

Besides industry-level regulation and demand growth, an important factor in corporate performance is the life cycle of the company and its consequent current position in the industry's growth profile. Many of the most successful companies in the CalPERS sample in the study's time frame (e.g., Intel, Home Depot, and Wal-Mart) were at an early stage in their development. They had new products, services and processes, and had high value-added whether or not 'good' governance practices were being utilized. In many cases, the corporate founders remained in charge and owned significant shares, so that these companies did not encounter agency problems, and there was less pressure on the board to protect the interests of shareholders. In addition, there was a selection bias involved in including newer firms in the sample. Almost by definition, any company that emerges as the survivor from the hundreds of new enterprises begining service in any given year will have superior management and is likely to experience greater growth. Thus, irrespective of board practices, newer companies in the sample of the largest in the economy are likely to realize better economic performance than that of older companies.

## The calculation of economic value added

We generate the value added for each year by subtracting WACC from ROIC. The one-year values are then indexed over the entire time period by calculating a weighted average using companies' total assets as weights to represent the financial performance over the period 1991–2001.

Once the series for each company is generated, the company is assigned to one of 14 industrial groups. We chose to separate regulated electrical and telecommunications utilities from electrical equipment and unregulated telecommunications firms and to eliminate the regulated companies from the sample. For each industry, average values are generated for each year's ROIC, WACC and value added. We then create a set of 'differential' values of ROIC, WACC and value added to represent the difference between each firm's performance in these respective categories and the industry average generated by the sample.[40]

The resulting valued-added performance for each company, versus its CalPERS grade for 1991–2001 is shown in Figure 5.1. The set of companies that received an A+ grade from CalPERS realized the largest positive

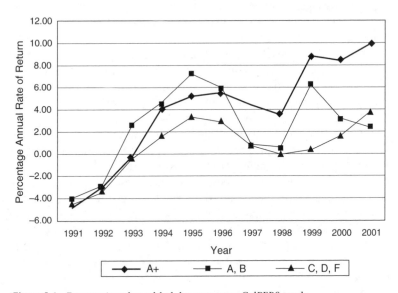

*Figure 5.1*   Economic value added, by company CalPERS grade

---

40  This procedure consists of the following sequence:

- derive values for WACC and ROIC for each firm over the 11-year period
- derive differences for each firm for each year
- for each CalPERS grade finds the [weighted] average differential value added for each year.

EVA™. Firms that received the two sets of lesser grades performed between 1.37 per cent and 3.16 per cent less well, on average, in excess return on operations over the same period. Only in 1991 did companies rated CDF fare marginally better than A+ companies, while in most years AB companies did substantially better than CDF companies in generating excess value added.

These results do not account for the industry effects. The first method for accounting for industry effects is to develop a counterpart to Figure 5.1 for estimates of percentage economic value added based on the differential spread for each company as indicated in the previous two paragraphs. This chart is shown as Figure 5.2. The 'A+ to other' difference for the last half of the 1990s is much more extreme; while A+ demonstrates differential economic value added in the range of 2 per cent, both AB and CDF have zero or negative differential spreads for the entire period.

Another way to account separately for industry performance is to develop a regression analysis of returns using all year-to-year data for the individual firms in the sample. The analysis disaggregates the data and attempts to filter out the effects not only of industry, but also of the 1991–2001 business cycle. We test the null hypothesis that, after

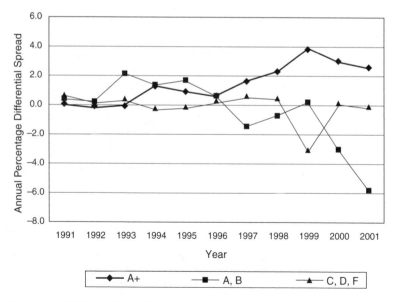

*Figure 5.2* Differential spread, by company CalPERS grade

accounting for other factors, no relationship exists between an individual company's performance and the existence of a higher grade for governance.

Determining the sample for this analysis mirrors the process for that developed in our assessment of average value added in Figure 5.1. Regulated utilities and financial services firms were removed from the database, as were combinations of year and firm for years in which particular firms did not operate. Appendix A details other firm-specific adjustments made to the data, due to merger activity. We define economic value added as the dependent variable and the following sets of (0,1) independent variables.

1  Year: 1991, 1992, 1993, 1994, 1995, 1996, 1997, 1998, 1999, 2000, 2001.
2  Industry: aerospace, automotive, chemicals, computers, electrical equipment, foods, health care, machinery, metals, miscellaneous, oil/gas, retail stores, telecommunications equipment, transportation.
3  CalPERS grade: A+, A or B, and C, D, or F+ (firms graded F were excluded from the study; firms graded F+ were relabelled as F). The form of the equation expressing a relationship is as follows:

$$\text{Company Excess Earning} = \text{Constant} + \Sigma \text{Coefficient}_i \times \text{Year}_i$$
$$+ \Sigma \text{Coefficient}_i \times \text{Industry}_i + \Sigma \text{Coefficient}_i \times \text{Grade}_i{}^{[41]}$$

Table 5.1 provides the results from testing the null hypothesis that high CalPERS grades for a company's board governance system do not add to a firm's economic value added. The fitted equations indicated that A+ companies, which form the base sample, have higher EVA, since AB companies realized EVA of 3.38 per cent less and CDF companies realized EVA of 2.75 per cent less. These results, with the AB coefficient significant and the CDF coefficient marginally insignificant lead to rejection of the hypothesis that higher CalPERS grades are not associated with greater return throughout the 1990s.

---

41  It should be noted that in specifying the equation, it is not possible to include all variables. For example, including the variables for 2001, when variables for 1991–2000 and the constant are already included, would result in multicollinearity. Therefore, we had to exclude one year, one industry and one grade group from the set of explanatory variables. We used the year 1992, the metals industry and the 'A+' CalPERS grade as the baseline, and thus eliminated them from the equation.

*Table 5.1* Equation for single company economic value added versus CalPERS grades on board activity

|  | Coefficient | Standard error | t-*value* |
|---|---|---|---|
| Constant | −12.192** | 3.600 | −3.39 |
| 1998 | 4.352 | 2.716 | 1.60 |
| Automotive | 9.258** | 4.227 | 2.19 |
| CalPERS Grade A, B | −3.381** | 1.423 | −2.38 |
| CalPERS Grade C, D, F | −2.746 | 1.515 | −1.81 |
| $R^2$ (adj) (%) | 11.1 |  |  |

*Note*: Sample size = 128. All figures are percentages. Statistically significant coefficients at 5 per cent level are denoted by **.

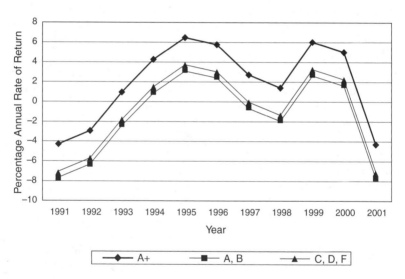

*Figure 5.3* Economic value added, by company CalPERS grade, accounting for industry effects

Figure 5.3 uses the regression to illustrate the differences in rates of return for grade levels by year, based on the coefficients for the grade AB variable of −3.381, which we consider statistically significant, and of the CDF variable of −2.746 which we consider to be not statistically significant. The lines take account of industry effects on returns (shown in the Appendix for the complete equation, as illustrated in Table 5.1 for automotive). Most illustrative is an example of a difference between

*Table 5.2* Comparative economic value added in the better- versus worse-governed stylized company (spreads in percentages; capital and returns in $ millions)

|  | 1991 | 1995 | 1998 | 2001 |
|---|---|---|---|---|
| Spread A+ stylized firm | −4.278 | 6.47 | 1.415 | −4.278 |
| CDF stylized firm | −7.026 | 3.722 | −1.333 | −7.026 |
| Difference | 2.748 | 2.748 | 2.748 | 2.748 |
| Average capital for that firm | 51,049 | 61,246 | 75,848 | 83,208 |
| Excess return A+ firm | −2,184 | 3,963 | 1,073 | −3,560 |
| CDF firm | −3,587 | 2,280 | −1,011 | −5,846 |
| Difference in investor returns | 1,403 | 1,683 | 2,084 | 2,286 |

two hypothetical companies, one rated C and the other rated A+. To have been a C-rated company rather than an A+-rated company, in CalPERS governance terms, was to have realized returns of 2.75 per cent less per year on average (as shown in Table 5.2).

A hypothetical C firm in the automobile industry, with capitalization equal to that of the average for all automotive firms in our sample, would earn $1,403 million less in 1991, and $2,084 million less in 1998.[42]

This would indicate that there have been significant increases in economic profit where a professional board was present. Although the results do not prove causation, corporations with active and independent boards appear to have performed better in the 1990s and early 2000s than those with passive, non-independent boards.

What, then, are the results of our inquiry? There is little doubt, we believe, that an active board aligned with shareholder interests would attempt to enhance value to shareholders. It is unrealistic to think that singular changes in board structure alone, without accompanying activist practices and policies in place, would make that kind of affect on corporate

---

42  When observing these results, one should bear in mind that, although one would intuitively expect greater economic return during a year of superior market performance, the relationship is somewhat more complex. Thus, while the underlying causes of a stock market boom may also drive increased sales and profitability, the resultant greater return on the market increases the opportunity cost of capital. Since the relationship between firm and market performance is incorporated into the firm's cost of capital calculations, these effects should balance out to zero over the long run. (Thus, the $6 billion represents the excess gains delivered over five years by the superior governance system in the A+ firm.)

performance possible. Thus, we have identified a surrogate for board's incentivizing and monitoring management performance in the 'graded' responses to the CalPERS survey. Those corporations in which the A+ grade as a surrogate for professional board behaviour was present, had superior corporate performance as measured by earnings in excess of costs of capital over the industry average.

There appears to be a substantial and statistically significant correlation between an active, independent board and superior corporate perform-ance. Moreover, we believe that the superior performance is a result of activist corporate governance. However, we recognize that a correlation between governance and performance does not prove causation but, even without proof of causation, it can be inferred that managers willing to assume the risks associated with a professional board are better able to generate higher returns to shareholders. On the other hand, could the causation go the other way? It seems to us less likely that good corporate governance is the choice of managers that on their own initiative have the corporation performing extraordinarily well.

## Superior performance after a change in governance

At the conceptual level, a change in governance with the installation of an active, independent board of directors results in a newly refocused management formulating superior competitive strategies and imple-menting these strategies for better financial results.

In pursuit of causality between governance and economic performance, we have developed the further hypothesis that changes in governance precede changes in economic value added: that is, good governance causes improved value added performance. For each company that received an A+ grade in corporate governance an attempt has been made for the period 1989–95 to find an event that initiated its reform in governance practices. Such events, for example, would include the discharge of a CEO and then the appointment of a new CEO, a restruc-turing of the board of directors, or a restructuring of governance in the face of a potential takeover. There was information available indicating such changes for 29 out of the 56 companies that received A+ grades. For these 29 companies, we created a variable that has a value of zero for all years before the event and the value of one for that year and all years following. For 12 of the companies that variable is equal to zero for all years, as no event occurred in the specified period; for the remaining companies this variable is equal to one for all years in the sample for any event that occurred before 2001.

*Table 5.3*  Regression equation for single company economic value added versus board change

| | (1) | | (2) | |
|---|---|---|---|---|
| | *Coefficient* | *St. error* | *Coefficient* | *St. error* |
| Constant | 3.467** | 2.355 | 3.438** | 2.355 |
| Chemicals, oil/gas | −8.858** | 2.924 | −8.857** | 2.920 |
| Aerospace, computers, telecom equipment | −9.097** | 2.935 | −9.053** | 2.937 |
| Retail, foods | 5.844** | 2.782 | 5.888** | 2.782 |
| Miscellaneous | −8.742** | 3.031 | −8.700** | 3.032 |
| Board change | 4.687** | 2.309 | 4.158** | 3.047 |
| Trend change | – | – | 0.1645 | 0.735 |
| Year One | −2.865** | 3.676 | – | – |
| Year Two | 1.974** | 3.676 | – | – |
| Year Three | 1.028** | 3.676 | – | – |
| $R^2$ (adj.) (%) | 18.2 | | 18.5 | |

*Notes*: Sample sizes are 29. All figures are percentages. Top number is the coefficient for the data; standard error (st. error) is listed underneath. Statistically significant data at 5 per cent level are denoted by **.

An equation for individual company economic value added, as determined by new board change, is described in Table 5.3. The independent variables in the first regression are the board change variable, which equals either 1 or 0, and three dummies, for Years One, Two and Three. Each of these is equal to 1 if the board change occurred a corresponding number of years earlier, and 0 otherwise. The fitted first set of coefficients indicate that a company that had a change in corporate governance operated to produce $4.68 - 2.87 = 1.81$ per cent higher economic value added in the first year after the change, 6.66 per cent higher in the second year, 5.71 per cent higher in the third year, and 4.67 per cent higher in all consecutive years. The second set of coefficients, with the time trend also adjusted for changes in governance, indicates that the first year average increase was 4.16 per cent, with subsequent years increasing by 0.16 per cent a year.

This implies that in the first year after the change, for example 1992, an increase in value added takes place equal to 4.16 per cent + 0.16 per cent = 5.32 per cent; in the second year it is 5.32 per cent + 0.16 per cent = 5.48 per cent and so on. In the first case, these year-to-year changes are significant; the implication is that activation of the governance process precedes improvements of earnings performance, at least in a subset of the largest corporations subject to a type of shakeout early in the subsequent period.

## Conclusion

The findings here are that the domestic large corporations with better governance systems, A+ graded according to company responses to CalPERS generated significantly more excess returns over the 1990s than similar corporations with not better governance systems. A subset of these better governed corporations after governance reform increased these excess returns. Good governance has improved economic performance where it has been adopted among the largest corporations in the mid- to late 1990s.

In earlier chapters we concluded that major structural reforms had been initiated before 1990, and this set of findings would seem to follow – the structural reforms in governance were followed by exceptional gains in earnings. There was reason to believe that boards of directors had moved beyond passive acceptance of management and become more 'professional' and 'activist' in evaluation of its performance. In Chapter 6 we contend that this expectation was premature and that the system did not have the capacity to keep the corporation on track to higher earnings when the economy in overheated. In Chapter 7 we believe we provide many if not all the further reforms necessary to complete another major correction.

# 6

## 'Where Was the Board?' Share Price Collapse and the Governance Crisis of 2000–2002

*Paul W. MacAvoy*

The last half of the 1990s was a period in which the economy expanded at a rate in excess of long term growth rates, due principally to investments in technical change resulting from new Internet and communications products. The promise of these products had beneficial effects across industry and trade, so that there was a balloon-like increase in share prices through much of the economy. By 2000 share price increases had, according to many financial analysts, developed into an authentic 'bubble'; but this was not long lasting, and inventory accumulation and other over investments brought the economy down by the end of 2001.

For shareholders, prices in Internet and communications stock could no longer be based on aggressive expectations of rates of growth of earnings far in excess of those of the last few years. While share prices by the end of 2002 had declined by more than 25 per cent, those of the new Internet and telecom companies declined by at least twice that percentage. With share price growth cut off, and cash flow from product sales declining, new Internet-based companies slid rapidly into insolvency. The largest companies in the economy, with stronger but still declining market demands, cut back on operations to levels that could be sustained by reduced cash flows and borrowings in debt markets. Their share prices declined, as prospects for future earnings were reduced in both the high-tech and investment sectors of the economy as a whole. The American economy went into one of its periodic slowdowns, not quite a recession, but this time marked by virtual collapse of these previously 'high expectations' sectors. The decline in the stock market across the board was sharper than in previous slowdowns because of the complete collapse of prices in those sectors.

Part of the collapse was due to a new phenomenon that overtook what was essentially a business cycle process, at least according to the media involved centrally in reporting economic events. A number of the largest corporations subject to this slowdown made extraordinary efforts to forestall the negative effects on their share prices; these efforts not only involved short-term reductions in operations but, in a surprisingly large number of cases, involved misleading and even fraudulent financial reports. In instances where this succeeded, for a limited period, in sustaining the artificially-high share prices, management cashed in its options and shares. The SEC subsequently initiated proceedings to determine the extent of securities laws violations in misrepresentation of the financial condition of those corporations, and in self-dealing, in that period.

The question is why was reform governance not there to stop the misrepresentation clearly not in the interest of the shareholders, that is, 'Where was the board of directors?' When management of these corporations went beyond coping with reductions in markets to self-survival action plans that drove the corporation into illegal practices did the board of directors know or could have known, and have prevented management from proceeding as it did. To search for the answer, we begin with an appraisal of the state of governance across all the largest corporations at the end of the century. We continue with an appraisal of compensation systems widely adopted in the 1990s for incentivizing management to focus on the performance of the corporation. These systems should have caused management to allow share prices to fall to sound levels. Then we attempt to find commonalities in the patterns of failure of those systems, and the board's failure to take control, for a sample of those companies subject to SEC investigations. Here in Chapter 7, given what we then perceive as the continued problem in governance systems, we propose solutions to this current crisis for the corporate form of enterprise.

## The status quo in corporate governance in the 1990s

If in the late 1990s the 300–500 largest corporations were once again surveyed to determine whether reform governance was functioning, the percent positive response would probably not differ from that in the CalPERS survey: that is, the response would have been mixed, from approximately 30 per cent that practised a strong form of governance to another 50 per cent that was moving towards a de facto shift of control from management to the board of directors. The 133 corporations that responded to the CalPERS survey included 56 which indicated that their governance practices centred on an independent board monitoring and incentivizing management to set out plans and programmes which enhanced gains to shareholders. Another 32 indicated that they were putting such practices in place, but were in the process and had not yet arrived at that point. The companies that responded negatively, or did not respond, to the survey (approximately 45 companies) were in our judgment not in the process of establishing strong governance. By 2000 many more of the largest corporations had entered into this process, with the management of more companies responding to GM and CalPERS as a wake-up call by sharing responsibility with their boards of directors for performance and, when opportunities presented themselves, revising the agenda in their own way to lead to enhanced shareholder returns. Then what could have been expected of these corporations when financial stress was encountered in 2001 and 2002, and the corporation's over-valued share price was no longer sustainable? Would management under board direction move to protect the interests of investors by proposing steps to reduce share price? Would strong governance processes not lead to support of such decisions by the board, under the pressure of personal losses on option values for both management and board members as share prices fell? These questions were put to the test in the collapse of product and share markets in 2000–2.

## Incremental change

Before assessing the role of governance, however, we might ask why there was only limited movement towards universal adoption of governance reform in the last half-decade. For those with weak governance, reform promised financial gain: according to our calculations, in the previous chapter, at least, companies could gain more than 200 basis points of annual EVA™, by letting independent boards of directors do the task assigned to them in the corporate charter. A 'governance premium' could be shared with management in option and stock awards through the increase in share price. Management as well as investors could gain from reform.

This inducement is stronger if the management-dominated corporation is only generating average earnings in its industry, and that industry is expanding at 2–3 per cent per year (similar, for example, to metals manufacturing or chemicals). Under such conditions, internal cash flow in a leading company is insufficient to generate investment for expansion at a higher rate than that of the industry. And the greater the opportunity for implementing a superior strategy, especially in a company with a less than compelling previous earnings record, the stronger the case for governance reform.

Even so, the reversal of roles between management and the board of directors requires management to surrender authority. As reported in Richard M. Clurman's *Who's in Charge?*,[1] Donald S. Perkins, former CEO of Jewel Companies, had a checklist for CEO candidates starting with: 'If you had a choice, would you even have a board? Would you tolerate a board strong enough to say no to you and evaluate your performance?' If the candidate provided negative answers to these questions the board would have to give way on governance reform.

However, we assume that CEOs, as individuals, act in their economic self-interest (otherwise, there is no 'agency problem'). The central issue has been to align self-interest with that of shareholders. Jensen and Meckling specified the problem in striking detail,[2] that decision rights were controlled by management. The work of numerous analysts since has focused on management payment systems that align management incentives to use these decision rights in the interests of investors.

The granting of stock shares and options by the early 1990s was seen as the means for aligning managerial with shareholder interests. If corporate executives are major shareholders, then the actions they take to improve share price in their self interest would positively affect all shareholders. Mehran, in a sample of 153 manufacturing firms in 1979 and 1980, found better returns to equity the greater the percentage of executive compensation based on returns to equity and the greater the percentage of shares held by managers.[3] With the promise that excessive corporate diversification in the previous decade was the result of managerial control of governance,[4] Denis, Denis and Sarin found a strong negative correlation between diversification and equity ownership of top management.[5] Additionally, Mehran found, after examining 30 voluntary liquidations from 1975 to 1986, that higher levels of share ownership by management were associated with reductions in diversification.

1 Richard M. Clurman, *Who's in Charge?* (Whittle Communications, 1994).

2 Michael C. Jensen and William H. Meckling, 'Theory of the Firm: Managerial Behavior, Agency Costs and Ownership Structure', *Journal of Financial Economics*, 3 (1976), 305–60.

3 Hamid Mehran, 'Executive Compensation Structure, Ownership, and Firm Performance', *Journal of Financial Economics*, 38 (1995), 163–4.

4 For a complete discussion of the literature on this subject, see David J. Denis, Diane K. Denis and Atulya Sarin, 'Agency Problems, Equity Ownership and Corporate Diversification', *Journal of Finance*, 52 (1997), 135.

5 See ibid., 135–7, 158.

Voluntary liquidation, associated with inefficient diversification, was positively related to the percentage of shares held by the CEO and also positively related to the extent of CEO stock options.[6]

This was not to conclude, however, that new compensation-based incentive plans were sufficient to cause management to undertake strategies solely in the interests of investors. Jensen and Murphy asked whether the impact of management decisions on stock values was of the same order of magnitude as on management compensation. In 1990 they found that CEO wealth changed by only about $3.25 for every $1,000 change in shareholder wealth.[7] Such a trivial change in CEO wealth questioned the effectiveness of this compensation mechanism in generating investor-centred performance. They concluded, 'The empirical relation between the pay of top-level executives and firm performance, while positive and statistically significant, is small for an occupation in which incentive pay is expected to play an important role.'[8] They continue, 'The relentless focus on *how much* CEOs are paid diverts public attention from the real problem – *how* CEOs are paid. In most publicly held companies, the compensation of top executives was virtually independent of performance before the early 1990s. On average, corporate America pays its most important leaders like bureaucrats.'[9] Jensen and Murphy listed three mechanisms for reform: requiring CEOs to become owners of substantial shares of outstanding stock; structuring salaries, bonuses and stock options to provide not only rewards for superior performance but also penalties for poor performance; and making real the threat of dismissal for poor performance. In the early 1990s they found that 'the realities of executive compensation are at odds with these principles'.[10]

Hall and Liebman developed new evidence, however, in the mid-1990s that indicated the growing importance of stock-based incentives. Using data up to 1994, they find that that increased use of stock options resulted in CEO compensation that was much more sensitive to performance.[11] Where Jensen and Murphy found a small change in CEO wealth for

6  Hamid Mehran, George E. Nogler and Kenneth B. Schwartz, 'CEO Incentive Plans and Corporate Liquidation Policy', *Journal of Financial Economics*, 50 (1998), 320.

7  Michael C. Jensen and Kevin J. Murphy, 'Performance Pay and Top-Management Incentives', *Journal of Political Economics*, 98 (1990), 225, 226.

8  Ibid.

9  Michael C. Jensen and Kevin J. Murphy, 'CEO Incentives: It's Not How Much You Pay, But How', *Harvard Business Review*, 3 (May–June 1990), 138–53.

10  Ibid.

11  Brian J. Hall and Jeffrey B. Liebman, 'Are CEOs Really Paid Like Bureaucrats?', *Quarterly Journal of Economics*, 113 (1998), 653–92.

a change in firm value, from a hypothetical executive decision, Hall and Liebman demonstrated that CEO wealth changed 'by many millions of dollars for changes in firm value that are not at all uncommon'. In addition, 'Typical changes in CEO compensation are small relative to typical changes in firm value, but not small relative to typical CEO wealth'.[12]

While stock ownership had become more of an incentive for CEO–shareholder decision alignment, it was not the only incentive to be considered important. Management career advancement tied to performance was thought to be at least potentially effective in motivating managers to work for gains to investors. Fama argued in the early 1980s that financial incentives were not necessary since the managerial labour market disciplined managers through promotions based on performance.[13] Holmström developed this further, but found that while promotion as a disciplining device could be substantial it was not effective in motivating managers to work hard in later years of their careers.[14] Gibbons and Murphy did not disagree in finding that career enhancement had incentive effects:[15] 'the optimal package had to provide a combination of implicit incentives from career concerns and explicit incentives from compensation'.[16]

In practice, however, companies did not implement the Jensen and Meckling three-part combination in the 1990s. Hall and Liebman note that 'relative pay' was not significant so that variations in executive returns

---

12 Ibid.
13 Eugene F. Fama, 'Agency Problems and the Theory of the Firm', *Journal of Political Economics*, 88 (1980), 288–307.
14 Bengt Holmström, 'Managerial Incentive Schemes – A Dynamic Perspective', in *Essays in Economics and Management in Honor of Lars Wahlbeck* (Swenska Handelshögkolan, 1982).
15 Robert Gibbons and Kevin J. Murphy, 'Optimal Incentive Contracts in the Presence of Career Concerns: Theory and Evidence', *Journal of Political Economics*, 100 (1992), 468–505.
16 Ibid. However, based on their studies of CEO compensation contracts, they also noted that current pay should be most sensitive to current performance for workers close to retirement, for workers at the top of the corporate hierarchy (such as CEOs), and for workers in declining organizations. This builds on earlier work by Rosen (1986), who, in the context of elimination tournaments and promotion ladders, observed that the incentive to win in an early round can be big even if the prize for that round is small if it gains admission to subsequent rounds with larger prizes. Rosen (1986) is also pertinent to our discussion of CEO compensation because it stresses the importance of high CEO compensation relative to the compensation of other senior managers within the firm. Rosen observes: 'Contestants who succeed in attaining high ranks in elimination career ladders rest on their laurels in attempting to climb higher, unless top-ranked prizes are given a disproportionate weight in the purse.'

had been driven mostly by ups and downs in the stock market.[17] The value of options in the executive compensation package should have been based on how well that corporation's share performed relative to those of counterpart corporations. In general option prices were not adjusted in compensation packages to a market or industry stock price index to eliminate the effects of general price runups.[18] This was an obvious adjustment that boards failed to address. To speculate, if it had been addressed, then the adoption of options tied to firm performance with strike prices net of market fluctuations would have made it more likely that management would not take on high risk projects in an effort to sustain that company's stock price as the market declined.

We have argued at length that in the 1970s and 1980s, in the so-called 'first crisis' in governance, corporate diversification was carried to excessive lengths, at costs to investors that should be designated as a product of the agency problem.[19] A stock ownership plan for managers that faced that problem would have been one that caused management to resist acquiring one more company; as shown by Denis, Denis and Sarin, there was a negative relationship between diversification and equity ownership of officers and directors.[20] But that relationship was not properly established; indeed in our personal experience with boards, and particularly compensation committees, management resisted hedging of options in their compensation packages in order to eliminate the effects of stock market wide price changes.

There were possible missteps. There is evidence outsider dominated boards paid CEOs more. One explanation is that companies with strong governance were not allowing management to incur large expenditures on perquisites, from airplanes to corporate retreats, with the result that a package on record had more cash income and bonus but less record non-cash compensation.[21] However, other studies suggest that measures of board composition, such as the proportion of outsiders, are misleading indicators

17  Brian J. Hall and Jeffrey B. Liebman, 'Are CEOs...?'
18  Ibid. In other words, no adjustment was made for economic value added.
19  For a discussion of the literature on this subject, see Denis, Denis and Sarin, 'Agency Problems', 135.
20  Ibid. In addition, a number of studies of board monitoring of management suggest that board stock ownership incentivizes more effective monitoring. That is, alignment of director incentives to investor returns through stock ownership can also be important for ensuring monitoring of management.
21  Richard Cyert, Sok-Hyon Kang, Praveen Kumar and Anish Shah, 'Corporate Governance, Ownership Structure and CEO Compensation' (working paper 1997); Brian K. Boyd, 'Board Control and CEO Compensation', *Strategic Management Journal*, 15 (1994), 335, 340.

of whether there is strong governance. One study looked at the relationship between CEO compensation and the 'quality' of board composition,
and found that firms with 'poor quality' governance tended to pay their
CEOs more: that is, CEO compensation increased as the number of directors
appointed by the CEO increased, and as the number of directors over the
age of 69 and the number of 'busy' directors increased.[22] If this relationship
dominated incentive compensation then the process of governance reform
was not advancing in the 1990s. Surely, if CEOs were in general paid more
in companies with weak governance systems, by amounts that were significant, then reform of governance was firm-specific only.

To the same effect, passive boards were slow to fire CEOs, tending to
make that decision only after poor corporate performance; in fact, only
very poor performance for an extended period of time led to measur-
ably shorter CEO tenure.[23] Even then, the question was whether firings
in the 1990s themselves were an important signal of emergence of
strong governance. There have been a number of studies of stock price
reaction to announcements of CEO firings: if CEO discharge led to an
increase in stock prices then it might be inferred that governance
reform was in the process of development. However, the statistical relation between firing and stock price change was difficult to interpret
since announcements of discharge convey what is often conflicting
information to investors about the performance of the firm.[24] Scott and
Kleidon develop evidence that investors treated CEO firings as positive,
and that they increased share values;[25] and Denis and Denis find evidence
that, on average, firm performance improved after a CEO was replaced.
More specifically, they report that forced resignations of top managers
followed significant declines in operating performance and were then
themselves followed by improvements in operating performance.[26]

However, interpreting this pattern of behaviour is problematic when the
corporation has a board of directors with a structure implying that it could

22 J. Core, R. Holthausen and D. Larker, 'Corporate Governance, CEO Compensation, and Firm Performance', *Journal of Financial Economics*, 51 (1999), 371–406.
23 See Jerold B. Warner, Ross L. Watts and Karen H. Wruck, 'Stock Prices and Top
Management Changes', *Journal of Financial Economics*, 20 (1988), 461, 487–8.
24 See Sanjai Bhagat and Bernard Black, 'The Uncertain Relationship Between
Board Composition and Firm Performance', *Business Lawyer*, 54 (1999), 921–63.
25 See Kenneth E. Scott and Allan W. Kleidon, 'CEO Performance, Board Types,
and Board Performance: A First Cut', in Theodore Baums *et al.* (eds), *Institutional Investors and Corporate Governance* (1994), 181.
26 David J. Denis and Diane K. Denis, 'Performance Changes Following Top
Management Dismissals', *Journal of Financial Economics*, 50 (1995), 1,023,
1,029, 1,055.

be active and independent. Weisbach reports that boards with at least 60 per cent non-affiliated directors were more likely than other boards to fire a poorly performing CEO.[27] Yet others found no significant correlation between board composition and CEO tenure either during the low-merger period of 1989–93 or during the high-merger period of 1983–88.[28] But Geddes and Vinod, after controlling for other factors in board composition, found that firms with a higher proportion of outside directors replaced CEOs at a higher rate than other firms.[29] This reverses the causality between executive turnover and reform governance: if it took strong-form governance to initiate a firing, then a firing does not lead to better governance.

These mixed findings regarding the performance of governance systems can be supplemented by evidence that incentive structures have been important with regard to board decision-making, particularly on CEO firings. The greater the dollar value of outside directors' equity holdings, the more likely it was that CEO turnover took place in a poorly performing company.[30] Further, when directors had incentive-based compensation, and ongoing performance of the firm was poor, then the likelihood of CEO turnover was greater.[31] Farrell and Whidbee find that while some directors were likely to leave, following the removal of a poorly performing CEO, those outside directors with substantial stock ownership and no close ties to the outgoing CEO tended to stay on the board.[32] To explain this phenomenon, they observe: 'Removing a poorly performing CEO . . . is one of the most observable signs that outside directors can send to shareholders and labor markets about their effectiveness as directors.'

In all, we conclude that strong boards instituted incentive systems for management with new emphasis on options and shares, and these strong

27 See Michael S. Weisbach, 'Outside Directors and CEO Turnover', *Journal of Financial Economics*, 20 (1988), 431.
28 See Wayne H. Mikkelson and M. Megan Partch, 'The Decline of Takeovers and Disciplinary Managerial Turnover', *Journal of Financial Economics*, 22 (1997), 205, 223.
29 See R. Richard Geddes and Hrishikesh D. Vinod, 'CEO Age and Outside Directors: A Hazard Analysis', *Review of Industrial Organization*, 6 (1996), 1.
30 See Sanjai Bhagat, Dennis C. Carey and Charles M. Elson, 'Director Ownership, Corporate Performance, and Management Turnover', *Business Lawyer*, 54 (1999), 885.
31 See Tod Perry, 'Incentive Compensation for Outside Directors and CEO Turnover', unpublished manuscript available at http://papers.ssrn.com (July 2000).
32 Kathleen A. Farrell and David A. Whidbee, 'The Consequences of Forced CEO Succession for Outside Directors', *Journal of Business*, 73 (2000), 597–9.

boards evaluated the results of operations so as to lead to the discharge of managements that performed poorly. But weak boards also did some of the same, except they probably over-compensated management. The most acceptable way of doing so was with excessive options, a highly desirable result for the recipients in a fast-rising stock market where options receive the full benefit of the market increases. Weak boards also did, indeed, fire managers but frequently with full retirement compensation and too late to be of benefit to the performance of the corporation.[33]

Whether incentive systems for management to bring performance in line with investors interest were generally effective cannot be determined, but the levels of options and shares in compensation packages were out of line by the end of the decade. Management incomes were much more impacted by stock marketwide share price changes. Consider that in the largest 200 corporations the beneficial ownership of options/shares in 1997 by the CEO was $39 million on average, and was $118 million on average in 2001.[34] This threefold increase in four years was the result of rapid rates of increase in the number of options granted by the board of directors and of the more than 20 per cent increase in stock market prices each of these years. If corporate governance practice by a strong board was in the process of bringing option values in line with gains in the share price of that corporation relative to the market then the result should have been average executive beneficial ownership in the $50 million range. That is, in the absence of the stock market bubble and the presence of strong governance, the average compensation package would have been in the $50 million range rather than the $118 million range.

The general position of those seeking reform in governance was to seek linkage of executive pay incentives to corporate performance through more options and shares. There was increased external pressure to discharge CEOs in poorly performing companies, which brought about more managerial turnover and more change to a strong form of governance. But the strongest evolutionary process was the shift to stock prices to reward performance as options became the dominant element in executive compensation. The attention of senior management, particularly those with a five-year time frame, focused on when the stock price would be at its highest and what to do to prolong the period in which it was at that level.

---

33 Paul W. MacAvoy and Jean W. Rosenthal, *Cost Containment Strategies and Nuclear Plant Safety: The Experience at Northeast Utilities* (forthcoming) (2003).
34 Cf. Pearl Meyer Partners, *2001 Proxy Research* (New York, private distribution). The averages are taken after exclusion of the top and bottom two companies.

This evolutionary process, in what we believe was the right direction, went off track in the last half of the 1990s given how 'cheap' options became in rising share markets. The relative performance of this corporation to its competitors was lost for determining rewards in the compensation package. As a result performance took on new elements of risk in the largest corporations: as managements carried out complex financial transactions to take positions on future earnings that enhanced share prices. Management also used its large degree of freedom in reporting earnings from period to period to enhance share price. With the guidance of the 'gatekeeper' – the outside auditor – transfers of previous revenues from reserve accounts to current period operating revenues allowed 'smoothing' of income within a very wide range. Current payments for services were booked as operating costs or investments, whichever provided more support for a positive income statement. If a down period was in the offing, management reduced reserves for an additional year of earnings to be capitalized in share price.

Of course, to do all this was not a straightforward exercise. The extremes are taken as misleading the investor for the sake of propping-up current share price. The board of directors in a strong governance regime would decline to undertake much of this exercise on the grounds that the audit committee should not approve any such procedures for which it would be censored by investors at a later date. The gatekeeper may find that this range of applications of 'managed earnings' practice not consistent with generally accepted accounting practice. But the passive board and conflicted auditor had the tendency to go along with broader accounting 'smoothing' initiatives from a management that had become focused on extending the current high stock price for just one more full accounting cycle.

## The collapse of Enron and the others

As corporate governance practice in the late 1990s moved towards stock and options, to focus incentives for management performance, stock prices and these option values took off to unexpected heights. Option-based compensation, for executives of firms with $5 billion of revenues, rose from tens to hundreds of millions of dollars per year. Then, in a return to reality, in 2000–1, stock market declines of 25 per cent or more caused executives to lose on options enough that compensation was negative. Management in numerous cases undertook to maintain the share price, against the interests of the shareholders in the corporation.

When their misleading activities were revealed, investors led a collapse in share price that in turn triggered debtor demands for payment with adverse effects on corporate liquidity. The resulting collapse, in at least a dozen of the largest corporations, raised the question as to whether there was a failure of corporate governance. Management self-dealing had involved misinforming shareholders as to the true condition of the corporation, causing share prices to be too high. That was supposed to be discovered, rejected, and penalized by the board of directors.

The torchbearers on this road to destruction were managements and boards at Enron, Global Crossing and WorldCom, three corporations with share prices above $60 in 1999 and below $1.00 in 2002. Each was an organization with assets worth from $30 billion to $100 billion. In the last half of the 1990s, their revenues had increased rapidly while earnings and cash flow did not increase as rapidly, and in some periods were actually in decline. Most significant was the fact that all three companies had negative economic value added as early as 1999 (see Table 6.1). Enron's losses against EVA™ increased over 1999–2001, from 4 per cent to 15 per cent. WorldCom never had positive economic value added in this period, which was dominated by its acquisition of MCI, making it the second largest long distance carrier in North America. Worldcom's economic value added fell from −14 per cent in 1999 to −23.4 per cent in 2000, and it then reached as high as −1.3 per cent in 2001. Global Crossing was a disastrous performer, with −21.1 per cent in value added in 1990, falling to −30.1 per cent of value added in 2002.

In each of these enterprises, management allegedly engaged in accounting adjustments and business transactions which were intended

*Table 6.1*  Economic value added at Enron, WorldCom and Global Crossing

| Company | Percentage value added (%) | | |
|---|---|---|---|
| | *1999* | *2000* | *2001* |
| Enron | −3.9 | −5.5 | −15.2 |
| WorldCom | −14.0 | −23.4 | −1.3 |
| Global Crossing | −21.1 | −14.2 | −30.1 |

*Source*: Based on corporation publicly announced financial statements, as compiled by COMPUSTAT™ estimation procedure as described in the previous chapter. Note that these estimates are based on public financial statements before a restatement corrected fraudulent reporting.

to create the impression of sustained high-level performance in their public income statements. While economic value added was negative and falling, the Enron share price doubled, from $24 to $48 in 1999, and then increased to between $60 and $80 in 2000. WorldCom's value added fell from −14 per cent in 1999 to −23.4 per cent in 2000 while its share price rose from $40 to $50 in that two year period; its value added then improved to −1.3 per cent but its share price fell to the $16 range, to be sustained at that level until it collapsed in mid-2002. Global Crossing at −21.1 per cent valued added saw its stock price increase from $20 to $40 per share in 1999; it then maintained that share price level until stabilizing at $25 through most of 2000. Given that economic value added was at −14.2 per cent in 2000 and −30.1 per cent in 2001, the stock price first increased and then went to zero in 2001 on the announcement of bankruptcy proceedings.

Over these three years, for these leading companies, economic value added declined while share prices were steady or increasing. The investor was grievously mistaken or grievously misled. There were product market indications that each of the three was in trouble. All three corporations incurred deep and sustained reductions in demand for key products in 2001.

Enron lost two-thirds of its expected trading volume in telecoms broadband capacity and half the accounting value of its long positions in gas contracts after sharp reductions in natural gas prices. It had used 'mark to market' values of gas contract positions from the previous year's high gas prices as book income to finance new ventures. While the necessary markdowns in book values of gas contracts were slow in coming in 2001, they could have been apparent to the knowledgeable investor. What was not apparent was the importance of (gas and electricity) trading for corporate earnings in what was reported as income. Gas trading was sharply reduced after the January–March 2001 price peak – the highest ever – and electricity trading was affected adversely by system shortages and the aftermath of severe price spikes in the new California spot market. In 1999, Enron trading was the source of almost all corporate earnings, as revenues from other operations were matched by the expenses of those activities and general expenses.[35] In the year 2000, trading generated more than $3 billion in

---

35  Testimony of Frank Partnoy, Professor of Law, University of San Diego School of Law, Hearings before US Senate Committee on Governmental Affairs, 24 January 2002, 11.

earnings, which covered losses of almost $1 billion in other wholesale operations. In 2001, before bankruptcy, reduced trading activity did not generate reported earnings.[36]

But the Enron public reports were confined to only that part of its operations that had been consolidated for purposes of constructing the public income statement and the balance sheet. Enron was involved in numerous off-balance-sheet partnerships, share trusts, hedging contracts, and prepay transactions which involved liabilities outside that were imperfectly hedged. Enron transactions with these entities and in these contracts increased its reported earnings and reduced its liabilities relative to those shown on the public financial statements. If these entities had been included in Enron's audited financial statements then Enron's reported earnings for 2000 would have been 28 per cent less. Enron's statement of cash flow from operations that year was shown as $3.0 billion when it was negative $153 million; its cash flow from borrowing was not $573 million but was more correctly $5.1 billion. The corporation in its November 2001 presentation to analysts in New York city estimated the liabilities incurred from these off balance sheet transactions were more than $25.1 billion, increasing total liabilities from $12.9 billion to $38.0 billion. (As a result, had these off balance sheet liabilities been included, debt to total capital ratio would not have been 40 per cent but 68 per cent).[37] The investor was misled by accounting for the sale of off balance sheet assets because the sale prices to the special purpose entities were in excess of the fair market value of these assets, which in turn generated excess revenue and led to the overstatement of Enron's operating income.

Global Crossing experienced sharp reductions in demands for telecommunications in its fibre-optic trunk lines, which is consistent with the downturn of the Economy after 2000. Management attempted to sustain the perception of continued high-level performance, however, through aggressive accounting for sales revenues, including revenues from circular buy-sell transactions with other trunk-line service providers on which there were no earnings. Founded in 1997, the

---

36 No final 2001 financial statements have been released by Enron. This estimate is from the author's extrapolation of CS First Boston analyst's estimates of 26 January 2001 (cf. 'Enron Corp., ENE "Strong Buy"', 26 January 2001, by Curt Jaunier, CS First Boston Corporation).

37 According to the Batson Report to the Enron Bankruptcy Court as reported in 'Enron's Real Financials' (Forbes.com, 3 February 2003).

company's strategy was to build undersea and landline fibre-optic capacity in anticipation of large increases in demand for Internet access, and to service at wholesale the regional Bell operating companies as they began to offer long-distance service as allowed by the 1996 Telecommunications Act. The company was financed with high yield bonds and bank debt; after it went public in 1998, with high leverage, its stock was highly over-valued at over $10 billion, based entirely on prospects of future earnings from these expansions. In the next two years Global Crossing acquired other telecoms (including Frontier and IPC/Ixnet) using more paper financing. Then the company's prospective future revenues declined sharply in 2001 during the sharp industry demand downturn, and the retarded entry of the Bell companies into long distance. In that process the investor was misinformed by reports of increases in revenue and optimistic forecasts in part sustained by capacity swaps with other carriers that allowed it to report increased sale revenues. The business purpose for swaps was to plug gaps in networks – too much USA–Asia capacity was traded for not enough USA–Europe capacity – but other swaps allowed the delivered capacity to be booked as revenue, and the received capacity to be treated as a capital expense. In the first nine months of 2001, these swaps accounted for $660 million, or most of the reported growth in sales revenues.

WorldCom in its MCI division was the largest carrier in business long distance telephone services in the domestic US market. It generated substantial cash flow until falling demands for service industry-wide in 2000–1. In the most misleading financial report of any large corporation, it resorted to shifting billions of dollars of direct expenses out of operating costs to investment. While the source of growth for Global Crossing had been an open line of debt capital, for WorldCom it was the ability to acquire telecoms for a high-priced stock in issue after issue of more shares for assets in the mid-1990s. The direction and pace of WorldCom growth by merger was opportunist, up to and including the 1997 purchase of MCI. After that acquisition, the pace slowed, and then stopped because of antitrust agency concern with possible anti-competitive effects in long distance and Internet services from such mergers. To sustain a share price, based on high rates of corporate revenue growth, with acquisition forestalled, WorldCom resorted to shifting of reserves into revenues, generating false reports of revenues, and as a last resort 'converting substantial portions of its line cost expenses into capital items – [adding] approximately $3.8 billion improperly to income'.[38]

Do these three companies' strategies fit together into a 'new type' of performance? The strategies of all three companies focused on growth of revenues, with earnings to come later, to sustain previous large increases in stock prices. The high prices came from over-valuation in the stock market of high-tech and telecomms; as it became clear that sales and earnings were not going to increase, management turned to financial engineering to keep prices at levels consistent with those in 1997–2000. In 2001–2002 earnings fell, and all three corporations made irregular and possibly illegal adjustments in financial reporting intended to make investors believe that the financial condition of the company was better than it actually was. Enron possibly took accounting practices beyond accepted limits in prepay contracts with its own off-balance-sheet entities, by reporting future tax benefits that didn't exist, and by reporting as income bridge financings of assets sold to other off-balance-sheet entities for which it was the guarantor.[39] Most problematic was the strategic decision to move non-saleable assets off the balance sheet to joint venture companies in which the counterpart equity holder and manager was an Enron employee and in which the purchase price of the Enron assets was inflated. This added to Enron's income and subtracted from Enron's liabilities but only so long as the joint venture purchased asset maintained its inflated purchase price, or the hedging asset (Enron shares) maintained its value. Global Crossing went down the same path of aggressive management of earnings by inflating revenues from transactions in fibre capacity with other carriers in which each bought and sold the same amount at the same prices. To sustain the level of earnings, WorldCom capitalized expenses, reducing costs relative to revenues in current accounts. By this methodology for over-stating earnings in 2000–1, it was able to maintain the appearance of sustained profitability. Its peak share price was sustained by false information just when WorldCom executives were cashing in.

---

38 Cf. *First Interim Report of Dick Thornburgh, Bankruptcy Court Examiner*, 4 November 2002, *in re WorldCom Incorporated et al. debtors*, Case no. 02-15533(AJG). After WorldCom filed for Chapter 11 bankruptcy, the Southern District of New York Bankruptcy Court appointed Dick Thornburgh as Bankruptcy Court Examiner, to examine 'any allegations of fraud, dishonesty, misconduct, mismanagement or irregularity in the management of the affairs of [the Company] by current or former management, including but not limited to issues of accounting irregularities'.

39 Cf. 'Barons of Bankruptcy', *Financial Times*, 31 July 2002, 10, accompanying tables.

The intended effect in each case was to hold share prices for a year or two beyond what could be justified by accurate income statements. The inaccurate statements, crafted probably outside the range of accepted accounting practice, played a substantial role in inflating share prices. When revealed, the required restatement of income, involving billions of dollars of write-offs, led rating agencies to reduce debt to junk status which in turn called for bond repayments or increases in standby reserves on trading that could not be sustained. Given that sequence of events, it can be concluded that the deception caused the bankruptcy.

Before the bankruptcy, however, senior executives cashed in options or their other equity positions to the tune of tens of millions of dollars (see Table 6.2). These amounts were far in excess of those from other executives leaving large corporations and they were in the opposite direction from those of the common share investors. Investors had been misled, to lose all equity value. While management increased its wealth, the investor holding shares over the same period lost everything.

The executive team at Enron cashed in more than a billion dollars of their options, a few months before shareholders finished losing almost $19 billion. The three top executives in Global Crossing took out $781 million before shareholders in that corporation lost $9 billion. The management at WorldCom went into a process of taking out $165 million while shareholders lost $127 billion. Furthermore, the executives at WorldCom borrowed from the company to pay margin calls on leveraged holdings of company stock; as the stock price fell, in the downturn of 2000–1, these loans were not repaid. The company not only over-extended options to management but also in effect hedged the price risk for those borrowing against the share price. The appearance is that of management

*Table 6.2*   Management and corporation changes in valuation at Enron, Global Crossing and WorldCom

| Company | Reduction in stock value, 1999–2002 ($ billion) | Total executive option redemptions ($ million) |
|---|---|---|
| Enron | 18.8 | 1,058.0 |
| Global Crossing | 9.2 | 781.5 |
| WorldCom | 126.8 | 164.7* |

*Includes $77 million over three years for B. Ebbers, as reported in the Thornburgh Report (2002).
*Source*: Data from 'Barons of Bankruptcy', *Financial Times*, 3 July 2002.

securing personal wealth while contributing to the collapse of share price for the rest of the shareholders.

## The nine largest companies investigated for fraudulent financial reporting

Between mid-2001 and 2002, nine of the largest 100 corporations were subject to Security and Exchange Commission formal investigations for fraudulent financial reporting. This series of investigations took place during or soon after deep reductions in their stock prices, and in some cases as bankruptcy proceedings began.

The nine companies are listed in Table 6.3. In the period of (or preceding) financial collapse, they generated revenues over a range in excess of $10 billion (Williams) to slightly less than $100 billion (Enron). In most, these revenues in that last recorded year were not significantly higher than, or out of line with, previous levels. What is remarkable, however, were the low levels of recorded cash flow, or of earnings before interest, taxes, depreciation and amortization (EBITDA). The average net cash-to-revenue ratio across these corporations was less than 7 per cent, and for Reliant and Enron it was close to zero.

Given low net cash to revenue levels the suspicion is that revenues had been over-stated; in fact eight of the nine corporations were then

*Table 6.3* Performance of the nine largest corporations under investigation in 2001

| Company | Revenue ($ billion) | EBITDA ($ billion) | Subject of investigation |
|---|---|---|---|
| Dynegy | 42.2 | 1.6 | Understated debt |
| Enron* | 139.6 | 1.7[†] | Overstating revenues |
| K-Mart* | 36.1 | 1.1 | Fraudulent accounting |
| Lucent | 21.3 | 13.7 | Pre-booking of revenues |
| Qwest | 19.7 | 7.3 | Capacity swaps |
| Reliant | 40.8 | 0.003 | Round trip trades |
| Tyco | 36.4 | 3.2 | Goodwill incorrectly accounted |
| Williams | 11.0 | 3.1 | Round trip trades |
| WorldCom* | 35.2 | 7.0 (3.6 revised) | Capitalized direct cost Accounts to over-state earnings |

*Seeking bankruptcy protection.
[†]*Sources*: Annual Report and 10K statements as reported to the SEC for the end of 2001, as indicated in the text. The subject of investigation as summarized by the authors. Estimates for Enron based on unrevised financial statements for nine months as reported in the *Batson Report*.

or thereafter accused of using questionable accounting methodologies to over-state revenues. Motivation was obvious – to indicate that revenues were constant or increasing, even if cash flow was not, played some role in artificially maintaining share prices. WorldCom went further, as we have seen, and treated operating costs as if they were capital investments, increasing reported net cash and investment outlays. This not only misled investors but also reduced shareholder gains since overstatement increased taxes on actual earnings.

Most of these corporations began to experience shortfalls in earnings against expectation beginning in 1999. Four of the nine had positive economic value added in 1999, with the rest experiencing negative value added that year (as shown in Table 6.4). But two of the four, Lucent and Qwest experienced sharp declines and had lost 44 and 13 per cent of their equity by 2001; by 2001 five of the nine had negative EVA™ and only Tyco and Reliant had sustained positive economic value added through the three years (based on public reports of financial statements, without later corrections).

For the nine corporations over this period, however, as declines in value added were realized, share prices did not similarly decline. Of the five with negative economic value added in 1999, three had large percentage share price increases in 2000 (see Table 6.5). We expect that share prices equal the expected value of earnings so that they will decline when earnings decline; it is exceptional in our experience to find lags of more than one

*Table 6.4*   Economic value added at nine corporations under investigation

| Company | Percentage value added (%) | | |
|---------|---------|---------|---------|
| | *1999* | *2000* | *2001* |
| Dynegy | −2.5 | 45.6 | 2.5 |
| Enron | −3.9 | −5.5 | −15.2 |
| K-Mart | −6.4 | −10.2 | −26.9 |
| Lucent | 9.4 | −12.3 | −44.0 |
| Qwest | 9.9 | 3.1 | −13.1 |
| Reliant Energy | 1.1 | 2.2 | 1.5 |
| Tyco | 10.1 | 3.7 | 8.0 |
| Williams | −0.9 | −2.8 | 5.4 |
| WorldCom | −14.0 | −23.4 | −1.3 |

*Source*: Estimates constructed as in Table 6.1, before restatements made in income statements required as a result of investigations referred to in the text.

*Table 6.5*  Shareholder returns for nine corporations under investigation

| Company | Stock prices ($) | | |
|---|---|---|---|
| | 1999 | 2000 | 2001 |
| Dynegy | 17.6 (122.2) | 56.1 (218.3) | 25.5 (−54.5) |
| Enron | 44.4 (55.5) | 83.1 (87.3) | 0.6 (−99.3) |
| K-Mart | 10.1 (−34.3) | 5.3 (−47.2) | 5.5 (2.8) |
| Lucent | 75.0 (36.4) | 13.5 (−82.0) | 6.3 (−53.3) |
| Qwest | 72.0 (11.4) | 40.8 (−43.2) | 14.1 (−65.4) |
| Reliant Energy | 22.9 (−28.6) | 43.3 (89.3) | 26.5 (−38.7) |
| Tyco | 39.0 (3.4) | 55.5 (42.3) | 58.9 (6.3) |
| Williams | 30.6 (−2.0) | 39.9 (30.6) | 25.5 (−36.1) |
| WorldCom | 53.1 (10.9) | 14.1 (−73.5) | 14.1 (0.1) |

*Note*: Annual percentage charges in returns are shown in parentheses.
*Source*: As estimated from COMPUSTAT™; percentage changes are all in total shareholder returns.

year. We suspect that efforts made to mask declining earnings with misleading income reports succeeded in keeping share prices artificially high.

Managements of these corporations by and large were able to cash in their options and/or shares before the stock price finally did decline. At Enron, as seen in Table 6.2, senior executives cashed in a total of $1.1 billion in shares and options. At Qwest, estimated cash out exceeded $2.1 billion for 12 individuals, including $1.5 billion for the CEO. At WorldCom, such cashing-in exceeded $164 million and at Lucent it exceeded $31 million.[40] In retrospect, management was incentivized to sustain high share prices for personal gain at the nine corporations. In the worst case, that of WorldCom, the Thornburgh Report found that when 'WorldCom's revenue figures did not meet or exceed the budgeted amounts the company would improperly increase revenues'.[41] The 'improper adjustments' caused revenues to be over-stated by at least $4.6 billion, and in the last half of 2000 'the company took the brazen and radical step of converting substantial portions of its line cost expenses into capital items ... [adding] approximately $3.8 billion

---

40 'Deals Within Telecom Deals', *New York Times*, 25 August 2002, business section 10; see also 'Bubble Beneficiaries'. Some of the listed transactions of options and shares for cash accrued more than a year before share prices collapsed for these companies.
41 *First Interim Report of Dick Thornburgh*, Summary of Initial Observations, 6–7.

improperly to income'.[42] While Tyco's share price was in the region of $30, later to fall to $10, the two top executives sold $510 million of shares.[43] Dynegy moved almost a billion dollars of debt of the balance sheet to a special purpose entity. Reliant sustained share price with round trip and wash trades that inflated revenues without generating earnings; investigations into these practices have not yet revealed whether management directly gained by option sales. In general, in the nine corporations, borderline accounting procedures were used to sustain the level of revenues and income reported on financial statements in a period when managements were redeeming their personal holdings of options, leaving shareholders to sell later after reporting had been corrected and share prices had fallen.

## Where was the board of directors?

Should not the board of directors have intervened, to inform shareholders of correct revenues and earnings, or to require management to correct misleading statements? This challenge to boards of directors was the reverse of that in the first crisis in governance. In the earlier crisis, management used shareholder returns to over-build the corporation, and depress share prices. In this period management used marginal and unacceptable financial accounting practices to sustain artificially high share prices. The reform of governance to solve the 1970s problem set newly independent directors to work finding incentives for management to increase price in the interest of the investor. Compensation committees of 'independent' boards of the largest companies undertaking governance reform granted stock options that increased the value of executive compensation packages particularly after shares reached full value.[44] Other corporations, reformed or not, followed the lead, and many boards of directors granted large numbers of options in a period in which all share prices increased by more than 20 per cent per year; if the grants had been made in share markets in which prices increased

---

42  Ibid.

43  *New York Times Business/Financial Desk*, 13 February 2002.

44  See, e.g. Allan Sloan, 'Accounting Reforms Won't Add Up Unless Stock Options Are Addressed', *Washington Post*, 14 May 2002, at E03 (citing as examples, Michael S. Dell, CEO of Dell Computers, who earned $2.6 million in salary and bonus, and options valued at $26 million; Tony Ridder, Chairman of Knight Ridder, received $935,000 in salary but was granted 150,000 stock options valued at $1.6 million).

at 5 per cent per year, these option grants would not have been excessive, but the combination of 'too many' at 'very large' increases in value had the effect of tying management totally to the inflated share price that resulted. From driving up undervalued share prices, the strong board was faced with overvalued shares.

The board of directors in each of these nine corporations saw warning signs of stress in corporate performance. Up to two years before stock price collapse, the nine were not generating earnings sufficient to recover costs of capital. The warning sign in revenue statements was the lack of sufficient earnings after taxes and interest to adequately return outlays on equity capital, which should have led the board in its periodic review of financial performance to an intensive analysis of financial conditions inside the corporation. The boards of directors of these troubled corporations did not undertake these investigations or issue statements to inform investors as far as we can determine.

At Enron, the board of directors knew (or could have known) that mark-to-market increases in gas contract values as spot prices increased would be reversed in the next year or two. They could have been briefed on how derivatives trading increased revenues but not earnings twenty-fold more rapidly than in other trading entities. Directors of other energy trading companies knew, since they discussed Enron's accounting for trades and either rejected or adopted the Enron techniques. Enron's board of directors was informed that the billions of dollars invested in capital ventures in India and South America were not providing earnings. The new start-up operations, water and broadband communications trading, were not meeting aggressive targets for growth set by the analysts. The board knew that trading earnings would not entirely cover the losses on 'physicals' such as the large foreign construction projects. But the key information that revealed Enron's real versus false assest-liability position was derived from the off-balance-sheet entities. They contained 65 per cent of Enron's total liabilities, or $25 billion out of $38 billion reported in the November 2001 restatement. The Enron sales of assets to off-balance-sheet entities was always profitable; the board of directors could have known that selling losing ventures at a profit to entities hedged with Enron shares could not sustain a positive net asset position. On five occasions at board meetings individual entities were discussed without reviews of the liquidity implications of all of them together.

At Global Crossing and WorldCom the boards of directors knew (or could have known) that new ventures in capital-intensive fibre-optic systems in North America would generate limited operating cash flow before the new century. Industry forecasts by 1998 began to perceive that competition from entering Bell operating companies in their long distance markets would lower their revenues and earnings. They should have realized that current earnings were principally derived from one-off events, including acquisitions or sales of capacity in fibre systems. These corporations were selling future earnings, or swapping revenues with other firms, to enable them to post transfers of assets as sales, and the concurrent receipt of similar assets of others as capital investments. The boards could have seen this 'churn' in their examination of financial working papers. The boards of directors could have asked whether that would stand as acceptable business practice if revealed in detail in the *Wall Street Journal* and when told that they were 'stretch' procedures they could have pursued them to a resolution to deny their use.

WorldCom's chief financial officer is alleged in SEC proceedings to have called for the transfer of billions of dollars of operating costs to accounts for investment expenses so as to allow the resulting earnings to meet analysts' expectations. These transfers were sufficiently complex not to be apparent to the board from examining working papers at a monthly board meeting. The board would not know unless an auditor or some other manager concerned with that practice brought that misapplication to its attention. But the audit committee could have asked, given that the (false) level of earnings was out of line with previous forecasts. The Thornburgh Report indicates that the audit committee was not asking the revealing questions: it 'did not appear to operate effectively or aggressively'.[45]

The question, then, can be amended: what could an independent board in a reform governance system have done? These corporations did not have reformed governance systems, in which aggressive independent behaviour would have filled the gaps in information and decision-making. In fact, Enron had an A rating in the CalPERS survey for being *in the process* of creating a board that would have the independence and resourcefulness to monitor this company. But this rating was a promise of future improvement, and (not unlike many other promises) it was not kept by Enron. Global Crossing and WorldCom did not take part in the CalPERS survey, both being in an early stage of formation when the rating exercise was carried out. Both corporations separated the chair from the CEO position, but did not have independent director committee meetings nor formal governance guidelines. These three corporations

---

45 *First Interim Report of Dick Thornburgh.*

in our judgment did not have standing at the 'A' CalPERS level: that is, the appearance good enough to pass as corporations with reformed governance without anything actually being done.

The six of the remaining nine corporations under SEC investigation did not have governance systems that merited ratings. Only one had any rating: an A for K-Mart, based on newly undertaking executive sessions of outside directors and adopting governance guidelines. The remaining five were unrated, as a result of not being selected or not responding to the survey. We can find only limited indication in the statements of these companies of board independence. Only Lucent indicated the existence of a separate chair which was reduced to senior director when the chairman returned to the CEO position. None of the five had indicated that board meetings were held in the absence of management. Except for K-Mart, none of these corporations held independent director meetings without management. Only K-Mart and Reliant had formal governance guidelines.

We infer that the managements under investigation for misleading investors were not in fact subject to strong or reform governance processes. The answer to 'Where was the board?' could well be that the nine corporations under investigation did not have independent boards with active and resourceful members able to ferret out the self-dealing behaviour that helped to bring down the corporation even if many had some of the structural elements that can lead to an independent and active board in place.

## A second look at management out of control

In this inquiry into the causes for the unravelling of acceptable management practice in 2000–1, there are two questions. The first has already been asked: namely, what went wrong in the governance process that allowed these results to be realized? Second, what could be done to change governance so that the next stock market downturn will not lead management to mislead investors? The Enron collapse is the 'hard case' that we think provides answers. What the board knew of management practices, what the board could have known, and could have been done are central to these answers.

Ideally, corporate governance systems should generate information and decision responsibility for the board of directors to prevent management from perpetrating fraud in financial statements. Advisers have a threshold role as 'gatekeepers,' in order to detect the unravelling process and reveal it at an early stage. The outside audit firm, and legal counsel on SEC matters, should be able to detect fabricated income statements in ongoing reviews of operational and financial accounting. They should make it clear when auditing practice is close to the edge of, if not outside, generally accepted accounting practice (GAAP). Once determined, they (together with 'inside' gatekeepers, such as the controller, corporate secretary and inside audit staff) should be involved in determining irregularities. And they should inform the board audit and executive compensation (i.e., performance) committees about their process of detection and what they find.

What went wrong at Enron to distort this process? There is no complete answer at this stage as multiple investigations are now under way of alleged violations of the securities and other regulations, but the large picture has been framed. There are two parts to a general answer, each having separate implications for further reform of corporate governance.

The first part is that the company was incurring losses in 2000 and 2001 not revealed in its reported income statements, and was probably insolvent while still showing significant equity in its reported balance sheets. According to an impressively detailed financial and accounting analysis provided to the bankruptcy court in the Enron proceedings (the Batson Report, Part Two of March 2003), Enron had negative cash flow from operations in 2000, and it had borrowed up to $5 billion because it did not have the cash to meet all its obligations that year.[46] We do not believe that the board of directors was aware of this condition, but it could have been, if the outside auditor, Arthur Anderson, and the board audit committee had been diligent and thorough in evaluating disaggregated information on income and cash flows.

Enron in 2000 posted revenues of $100 billion from energy production and distribution and from energy and telecoms trading (both domestic and foreign). Those revenues were probably expected to result in earnings at some later period. But there was an unstable balance between earnings on trading energy and on investments in new large power facilities. This was the third year in which core operations generated earnings of less than $500 million, corporate had losses of close to $500 million, and wholesale services generated earnings of more than $1 billion. Cash flow from energy and trading, and from borrowings through off-balance-sheet

---

46  Cash as a percentage of obligation was –0.70 per cent according to excerpts from the Batson Report in 'Enron's Real Financials', Forbes.com, 3 February 2003.

entities, were sufficient to result in overall operating cash flow of an estimated $5 billion.[47] But trading income was over-stated by an amount in the hundreds of millions of dollars, or else Enron was realizing profit margins on trading two or three times larger than those of any other company. Gains from transactions transferring assets to the special purpose entities were also greater than would have been realized from market sales; given that these transactions were funded by borrowings of the special entities and guaranteed by Enron, the liability of Enron was greater than the value of the assets. That there was no value added from trading is indicated by Enron's risk measure, the valuation of assets lost in the worst case trading scenario (VAR, defined as variant risks, at 5 per cent probability); by 30 September 2001 the VAR potential liability was equal to its trading assets as shown in Enron's 10K and 10Q statements to the SEC.

The cumulative impact of these management practices has yet to be revealed but it makes it probable that the corporation was insolvent in that year. The board was not aware of this cumulative impact but it could have perceived the buildup of these liabilities. It could have been informed of how close to illiquidity would be the result of calls for cash when investors and debt holders were made aware of the cumulative impact of these operations.

The second part has to do with management practices specific to the off-balance-sheet entities. In more than a dozen transactions in which assets were transferred (sold) by Enron to these entities over the 1998–2001 period the board of directors could have questioned management's fiduciary practices. Three requests by management for approval of new entities by the board spaced over two years should have raised flags on the extent of executive conflict of interest: these new entities were to be managed by Enron executives who would be spared losses on their own account. This made them on their face nontransactions, structured solely to remove assets from the balance sheet while incurring liabilities larger than them. But losses on specific projects began to accumulate by mid-2000 and continued up to November 2001 and each loss was reported to the board. Yet on expressions of concern by the board, the management response was

---

47 Cf. the table entitled 'Enron Corp and Subsidiaries 2000 Consolidated Income Statement', p. 11 of Partnoy's testimony. Almost all these revenues were accumulated late in 2000 from open positions in gas and electricity prices in California during the power price spike. Cf. 'Enron Papers Show Big Profits on Price Belts', *New York Times*, 12 December 2002.

that each was a special case related only to its own conditions and the unique conditions of the markets in which it was being offered. While the board likely concluded, understandably, that each was not fatal in and of itself, it could have seen that the pattern was that altogether they could indeed be fatal. The board asked, but when there was no management follow-through, they did not ask again.

The United States Senate Subcommittee, in its report on the *Role of the Board of Directors in Enron's Collapse*, found that 'the Board received substantial information about Enron's plans and activities and explicitly authorized or allowed many of the questionable strategies, policies and transactions now subject to criticism'.[48] The Enron board of directors objected to this characterization and responded with a letter which took the position that it had to 'rely on representations made to them by management' and 'if they had been provided with accurate information ...this tragedy would have been avoided'.[49] They relied on management reports that were misleading and incomplete. But our perception is that they did nothing in response to a pattern of high risk self-dealing by management that was obvious and called for proactive monitoring as well as periodic over all review of the whole set of such entities. The board's reviews appear to have been less than the appropriate response to fast-changing and worsening conditions. They could have been better informed, but they could have persisted with questions, rightfully asked, which were not answered, and become informed.

'What went wrong' was that management strategy, with board approval, attempted to shift assets from low risk, steady current profit energy distribution to energy capital projects and trading, both with increased risk and only potentially increased future profitability. Employees were motivated to generate additional revenues, and additional earnings, by taking on aggressive new market-creating opportunities. It called for taking half of corporate assets off the balance sheet and faulty hedge transactions to reduce the risk of long positions. When Enron became desperate it used Enron employees' shares to complete the other side of these transactions.

Enron became a classic illiquid (failed) new enterprise in markets that it in good part originated. It simply over-extended trying to sustain an

---

48   US Congressional Report, *The Role*, 13.
49   W.N. Eggleston, 'Letter to Senators Linus and Collins re: PSI Report No. 107-70 (Report of the Permanent Sub-committee on Investigations, *The Role of the Board of Directors in Enron's Collapse*, 8 July 2002)', 1 August 2002, Executive Summary.

$80 share price with $30 of assets. Its invention of new selling devices for disposable assets, the special purpose entities, extended the values of its positions of advantage from promising initial stages to project collapse. The investor lost not only the over-valued stock price but also the real value of operating assets.

What more, then, could have been done if it had in place an active board of directors, informed and able to anticipate the implications of each of the major steps in the strategy? Two years before bankruptcy, as the board was informed of expansions in trading activities, it could have required the audit committee to undertake risk management in such activities and to discuss with the board their assessments of the solvency and liquidity position of the corporation inclusive of off-balance-sheet activities. Enron was no longer a gas pipeline company, providing gas and transportation to retail distributors in the upper Midwest, and neither was it just trading primary and secondary space in gas transmission lines. When it moved into the new strategy it was not enough for the audit committee to have periodic reviews of the cash flow from the world's largest energy trading operation. If the board had known of the stagnant condition of non-trading activities and the risk in open positions in gas trading it should not have agreed to continue management's 'asset lite' strategy. It could have informed shareholders that Enron had become a commodities trading company burdened by low-performing physical assets in power plants and pipelines. An active and independent board could have focused its periodic appraisals of management performance on risk management, based on analytical briefings on future cash flows from shifting out of energy production into trading electricity, gas, fibre-optic trunk-line space, and water supplies.

In other words, strong governance by the Enron board of directors, armed with substantive information on the implementation of complex programmes to change the nature of the corporation, could have led to board decisions that at the least would inform shareholders as to the nature of the new Enron. Enron was a new commodities broker, not another utility pipeline. And the board could then have made decisions curtailing high-risk programmes that did not conform to the corporate mission, as determined by share price responses of investors.

It is still possible that, even with 'strong governance', a management with expertise in complex financial transactions could bypass the board, with practices that reduced equity value but increased management returns. However, we cannot tell in this instance. Enron did not have a strong governance process in place, and neither did the other corporations under investigation. But it is our position that the CalPERS 'A+'

rating governance process would have made a measurable difference in response to a management 'out of control'.

During the late 1990s, in a period of greatest pressure on corporate performance, because of over-valued stock prices, management at Enron and elsewhere had great difficulty in maintaining the appearance in financial statements that they were still on strategic growth paths for revenues and earnings that would sustain the over-valued share prices. Those managements that were in fact able to maintain the appearance, without the substance, engaged in accounting irregularities that tested and at times breached GAAP practices. It took deceptive transactions to puff up the income statement in line with stock prices twice too high. Responsive governance could still be effective however if the board knew and if the board acted to prevent these management 'stretch' activities. If the board could have known but was not informed because of a poorly functioning information system, or the board knew but did not act, then governance systems failed.

Our understanding, from concentrating on this subset of corporations with important legal problems, is that there are correctable faults in governance in that the board 'could have known' and then the board 'could have acted'. 'Could have known' can be transformed to 'knew and acted'. Substantial improvements in information systems in governance can and will lead boards to monitoring corporate performance so as to prevent irregularities that mislead investors. And 'could have acted' can be reduced further, to minimal levels, if the board is motivated to act aggressively against even the appearance of irregularities. We offer proposals in Chapter 7 by which governance can be extended to detect and eliminate wrongful management practice and to motivate the board so to act.[50]

These proposals will do more than ensure the board has the information necessary to recognize managerial misconduct and corporate malfeasance. They will enhance the board's ability to determine when taking a corporate action is simply too risky and not in the interest of the shareholders, as well as its ability to recognize a failing corporate strategy, or management's failure to execute an acceptable strategy. In this regard, the litany of recent corporate failures is instructive to the future of good governance.

---

50 Of course that does not include criminal behaviour such as theft or other forms of self-dealing which may be hidden from the most alert and aggressive board. The state courts and the SEC have to suffice in their enforcement actions or with expanded enforcement resulting from increased funding for monitoring and detecting these activities.

# 7

# Proposals for Reform of Corporate Governance

*Ira M. Millstein and Paul W. MacAvoy*

The faults in governance and ensuing corporate performance in two different eras, the 1980's conglomeration and the 1990 stock price loca-lations provide the basis for proposals that we believe will enable boards to monitor management more effectively in market downturns as well as upturns. We propose steps that will change lack of access to know-ledge to 'knew and acted' on that knowledge.

The first important initiative is for the board, with the prodding of list-ing requirements if necessary, to develop an identified independent leader-ship, by separating the roles of chairman of the board and CEO and appointing an independent director as chairman. Independent leadership is critical to positioning the board as an objective body distinct from man-agement and, in particular, to the board's ability to: (i) identify the issues it should focus on including, in particular, the strategic issues of importance; (ii) obtain the information it needs to assess management's performance against its chosen strategy, including the overall conduct of the business; and (iii) prevent any management efforts to obfuscate important issues or information needed thereby hindering the board's ability to fulfill its responsibilities. This is intended to further support effective management as much as to ferret out bad decisions and poorly functioning systems.

The mosaic of federal law, regulation and listing rules proposed, enacted and adopted that constitute the 'New Reforms'[1] provide a necessary founda-tion for more effective board monitoring but are insufficient for their failure to address the separation of the chairman and CEO, as set forth in greater detail below. The New Reforms are designed to improve director oversight

---

1 The reforms impact both foreign and domestic companies, although the reforms for domestic listed companies are more far-reaching.

of corporate affairs while reducing inaccuracies in the reporting of corporate financial performance, and embody in significant respects (primarily through the proposed listing rules) recommended 'best practice', including:

- a majority of independent directors;
- more rigorous standards for director independence;
- further restrictions on audit committee composition and additional responsibilities for audit committees;
- wholly independent compensation and nominating/governance committees and specific responsibilities for these committees;
- regular sessions of non-management directors, with a designated presiding director;
- regular board and committee evaluations; and
- company-specific governance guidelines and codes of conduct and ethics.

In addition to establishing a new regulatory scheme for public company auditors and mandating additional corporate reporting requirements,[2]

---

2 Sarbanes–Oxley §§ 201–209 establishes new standards for auditor independence; §§ 101–109 establishes a new regulatory process for public company auditors, and a new standard setting body. Sarbanes–Oxley also prohibits independent auditors from providing many of the non-audit services (other than tax services) that accounting firms typically have provided in the past. Enhanced corporate reporting requirements under Sarbanes–Oxley include: (i) annual management and independent auditor assessments of internal controls and required disclosures about these assessments (§ 404); (ii) additional disclosures concerning off-balance sheet financing and financial contingencies (§ 401); (iii) additional regulation of the use of pro forma financial information (§ 401); (iv) a requirement that all financial reports filed with the SEC reflect all material correcting adjustments identified by the Company's independent auditor (§ 401); (v) accelerated disclosure of director and officer stock transactions (§ 403); and (vi) new 'real time' disclosure requirements for certain information concerning material changes in a company's financial condition or operations (§ 409). Other important provisions of Sarbanes–Oxley provide for: (i) enhanced disclosures about potential conflicts of interest in security analyst reports (§ 501); (ii) requirements for lawyers representing issuers before the SEC to report evidence of material violations of securities laws or breaches of fiduciary duty or similar violations by an issuer or its agents to senior officials, and if need be, to the board of directors (§ 307); (iii) expanded SEC regulatory review of company disclosures, enhanced SEC enforcement powers and increased civil and criminal penalties for securities law violations (§§ 408, 3, 801–807, 901–906, 1,101–1,107); and (iv) additional inquiries by the SEC and other governmental agencies regarding the use of 'off-balance sheet financing' and special-purpose entities, credit rating agency activities and investment banking involvement in company financing arrangements (§§ 401, 702, 705).

the Sarbanes–Oxley Act of 2002 heightens or establishes new legal requirements as to responsibilities and ethics of corporate officers and directors
for SEC reports through several key mechanisms:

1 CEOs and CFOs are required to certify to the SEC that annual and
  quarterly reports are correct and complete 'in all material respects'
  and to certify that they are responsible for, and have evaluated, the
  internal control systems (with knowingly false certifications subject
  to criminal penalties).[3]

2 Companies are required to disclose in their periodic reports
  whether they have adopted a code of ethics for their CEO and
  senior financial officers, and if not, provide an explanation for not
  doing so.[4]

3 The application of rigorous independence standards for audit
  committee members.[5] In addition, audit committee must be granted
  enhanced responsibility for audit oversight, including authority to
  hire and dismiss independent auditors and to pre-approve all non-
  audit services to be provided by the independent auditor.[6] The audit
  committee must also establish a mechanism for addressing complaints concerning accounting and compliance with securities laws.[7]
  Greater disclosure is required concerning committee activities and
  responsibilities (including disclosure of all non-audit activities the
  committee approved the independent auditor to provide).

4 Personal loans by companies to their directors or executives are
  prohibited, other than certain customary consumer lending transactions (and, in the case of companies that are or own broker-
  dealers, margin loans to their employees).[8]

In addition to the Sarbanes–Oxley Act, both the NYSE and NASDAQ
have proposed significant amendments to their corporate governance

---

3 Sarbanes–Oxley § 906. See also Sarbanes–Oxley § 302 (requiring that a company's
  periodic reports include certain certifications by the CEO and CFO, subject to
  civil liability for fraud).
4 Sarbanes–Oxley § 406; Exchange Act Release No. 47235, 24 January 2003.
5 Sarbanes–Oxley § 301.
6 Sarbanes–Oxley §§ 201–202.
7 Sarbanes–Oxley § 301.
8 Sarbanes–Oxley § 402 (note that existing loans may continue but may not be
  materially revised or extended).

listing requirements.[9] As noted, these new minimum standards embody, in significant respects, what have been up to now recommended 'best practices' for listed companies. (The two sets of proposals have some differences, and different exceptions may apply.) Former 'best practices' reflected in one or both sets of proposals include:

• Requiring that boards be comprised of a majority of independent directors;
• tightening standards for director independence;
• further restricting audit committee composition and expanding audit committee responsibilities;
• requiring that compensation and nominating/governance committees be formed that are comprised entirely of independent directors and granted specified responsibilities;
• convening regular 'executive' sessions restricted to the non-management directors;
• requiring a 'presiding' director for such executive sessions;
• performing regular board and committee evaluations; and
• publishing company-specific governance guidelines and codes of conduct and ethics.

However these proposals are implemented, the requirements of the New Reforms focus more on board structure and disclosure than on conduct. In certain respects, they echo those parts of the GM guidelines which, though voluntary, instigated structural governance changes in a number of large US corporations. In our opinion, the New Reforms institutionalize many of the structural prerequisites to establishing an active and independent board, which also was the goal of the GM guidelines. However, as a result, they do not go far enough. First, the New Reforms are merely structural, and as the studies described in earlier drafts demonstrate, structure alone does not – and cannot – mandate the conduct that exemplifies an active and independent board. Second,

---

9 Corporate Governance Rule Proposals Reflecting Recommendations from the NYSE Corporate Accountability and Listing Standards Committee (16 August 2002, and subsequently revised 12 March 2003) available at http://www.nyse.com/pdfs/corp_gov_pro_b.pdf and at http://www.nyse.com/pdfs/2003-06fil.pdf, respectively. NASDAQ, 'Affected Marketplace Rules: 4200(a)(14), 4200(a)(15), 4350(c), 4350(d), and IM-4350-4', 9 October 2002, and subsequently revised 17 March 2003 available at http://www. nasdaq.com/about/2002_141.pdf and http://www.nasdaq.com/about/SR-NASD-2002-141-FED-REG.pdf.

even as a matter of structure, the New Reforms do not mandate a separate independent chairman, which, in our view, is the most important structural reform to institutionalize. We acknowledge that 'conduct' is too ephemeral for detailed legislation. But we believe the conduct we seek is far more likely with separate, independent board leadership devoted to the task of ensuring the board receives adequate information and focuses appropriate attention on critical issues, including strategic planning. As stated at the outset of this Chapter, the need for independent leadership derives primarily from the board's need to identify appropriate agenda items and have sufficient information to decide on those items.

We also acknowledge that Sarbanes–Oxley's requirement that the CEO and CFO certify the accuracy of company accounting statements, and their own responsibility and assessment of internal controls, mandates 'conduct', but this 'conduct' requirement does not extend to the board. We would add a requirement that the board determine to its own satisfaction that management's certification was based on an appropriate process. The board of directors should be required to take some responsibility to assure itself that management's certification has been accomplished with care and diligence.

This is a missing step in the Sarbanes–Oxley Act and other New Reforms. If, for example, boards support management strategies that involve complex hedging and financial accounting practices having the potential to mislead stockholders and enable managers to usurp corporate assets, then boards – under their duty of care obligations – should have to acquire the knowledge and monitoring skills to understand and approve the process used by management to certify that all is well. This would reinforce the board's interest in ensuring that it has all the information necessary to provide informed oversight which is a key element in the reforms we propose.

We suggest that managed earnings, 'financial engineering' and risk assessment be front and centre on the board's agenda, when relevant. If the practices we advocate were common, then early detection of questionable or illegal practices, and the imposition of penalties costly to out-of-control managements, would be possible. Detection is problematic given the sophistication of new and innovative hedging and risk management techniques. A variety of techniques to manage earnings are available for a management team that seeks to artificially prolong 'good news' on operational performance. Given the sophistication of many of these techniques, when they are detected, it is often delayed, which means that the board response now is further delayed, given that boards meet infrequently and decisions are made by consensus.

If the board is to monitor management effectively and hold it responsible for results, it must make a good faith effort to obtain the information it needs on an 'early warning' basis. This must be done. In the newly sensitized environment, relying solely on a single person (serving in the capacity of both CEO and chairman) to determine when to raise tough issues and how to package the information required for the board's evaluation may be considered (by the plaintiff's bar and some jurists) to be of questionable prudence.

Positioning the board to be knowledgeable, aware and active requires significant additional intelligence as to management and the business, as well as appropriately focused board agendas and meetings. This will not be forthcoming from a chairman who is also CEO. It is contrary to human nature to expect total objectivity from the CEO regarding his or her performance relative to strategies he or she has helped to formulate. Accordingly, we believe the chairman of the board of directors must be independent of management – even if only to ensure that the board has the information necessary to provide informed oversight. The board leadership role most clearly manifests itself in the setting of the board agenda; only the chairman can move a two-hour report on the last month's performance of the plastics division off the agenda to be replaced by a report on how that division and other divisions rank with respect to the volatility of revenues. The chairman has to present herself or himself as the agent for the board, in setting the agenda and obtaining necessary information for the board's deliberations on the performance of the CEO in implementing the corporate strategy. Unfortunately, in this regard, the New Reforms do not go far enough. While the NYSE proposal requiring a lead director to preside over executive sessions is better than the status quo, boards need the active independent leadership an independent chairman would provide on a full time basis.[10]

Accordingly, we make a number of proposals. Our imperative proposal is that the roles of chairman and CEO be separated. Our additional proposals for reform are close to an imperative; they are essential if

---

10 That the New Reforms fall short on the issue of independent board leader-ship is becoming increasingly apparent as companies begin to describe how they plan to comply with the proposed presiding director requirement. A number of large companies, for example, have announced that the director to preside over executive sessions will rotate alphabetically or according to seniority. This clearly will not provide the overall level of leadership for inde-pendent directors that we believe is necessary.

the board is to be capable of carrying out its complex role, and are based on the learning, history and experiences we have recounted up to this point.

First, priorities must be sufficiently formalized for boards to be sure that management has adopted reliable procedures to determine the accuracy of all public finance statements required by the Sarbanes–Oxley Act. This requires board members to know not only cash flow versus earnings, but also how and from which information system these estimates were derived, as well as the roles played by internal and external auditors in the validation of the information from which the estimates were derived.

Second, evaluations of management performance must be made by the board, as it always has been, but in this new era these evaluations must go beyond consensual conclusions that she or he is providing accurate financial statements. Boards should employ consistent measures over time to the effect that management is on track in achieving the preconceived goals of the corporation. The board should test and measure management against benchmarks linked to existing corporate strategies, which themselves have to be developed by the board in concert with management. A board fully involved in developing a five-year strategy for competitive advantage, with ambitious annual benchmarks for gains in sales and earning, and safety margins for unexpected cyclical changes, would have a significant foundation for determining whether management is performing at the requisite level. This procedure would replace engaging in the old annual forecast game with management proposing 'soft' gains in sales and earnings that with certainty are exceeded for purposes of awarding a full bonus by the end of the third quarter. But it does not imply setting a single-value goal from a linear growth line in a utopian strategy: too high an annual compensation goal is worse then too low a goal, since it provides incentives for inflating the financial statements. A board-led plan that sets the stage for flexible negotiation on executive continuity and compensation based on a strategy which, with uncertain gains and losses, maximizes the cash flow that accrues to those that capitalize the enterprise is the conduct we seek.

Our review of compensation plans and their observed connection to management performance in Chapter 6 did not promise the facile development of such a reward system. But the history of senior management cashing out its options while corporate share prices were over-inflated in the late 1990s makes it clear to us that compensation plans with large option holdings are not effective when all share prices double in a very few years. Board compensation committees should grant bonus awards only for the superior performance of that company relative to its competitors and options where strike prices are net of the effect of market wide value increases.

Our third proposal is closely linked to the second. Boards should assure themselves of the integrity of management, and compensation arrangements should reward extraordinary performance of dedicated leadership. When the share price is $100, not $50, and both board and management know it is over-valued, then concern for integrity should be heightened.

Fourth, boards should establish procedures to familiarize themselves with alternative strategies and innovative products, and structure their meetings so that issues central to the performance of the company are given sufficient time for the board to consider options, and not simply listen to reports. Also, as important, and we believe obvious, to further their access to information, the board should hire separate consultants or advisers it deems necessary in order to carry out its responsibilities.

We expect that, in addition to boards doing all this under the threat of regulatory and judicial pressure, change will come if shareholders, particularly institutional shareholders, press for these reforms in board conduct and the media continues to reveal transgressions and wrong-doing in cases centering not only on management but also board performance. As many have begun to ask recently, we should continue to ask, where was the board?'

## New expectations for improved performance in boards of directors

On the face of it, the New Reforms do not alter the basic fiduciary duties of directors. However, they do provide detailed mandates that have important legal implications for directors to consider carefully. Directors should be aware that highly respected members of the Delaware judiciary and other notable commentators have already predicted that the New Reforms will spark a wave of litigation involving claims for breach of fiduciary duty. These new claims – which will probably be brought in Delaware courts – will affect both inside and outside directors.

From mid-2002 to early 2003, the Delaware Supreme Court issued written decisions in five cases involving the performance by directors of their fiduciary duties. *In every one of these five decisions, the Supreme Court held for the shareholders and against directors*, reversing Court of Chancery decisions that had rejected the shareholder claims.[11] This recent jurisprudence suggests a shift in judicial expectations and the standards of conduct by which directors must act. As the Chief Justice of the Delaware Supreme Court, E. Norman Veasey, remarked at recent a *Harvard Business Review* Roundtable, there is 'a new set of expectations for directors... that is changing how the courts look at these issues'.[12] Given the current state of the corporate environment, we believe courts will recognize heightened conduct requirements for directors and impose liability on directors where those standards are not met.

In the wake of the sensitized environment resulting from the corporate failures and scandals of the past two years – and in light of the New Reforms – we envision state court litigation arising out of two principal areas:

- claims for breach of fiduciary duty (primarily duty of care) based on failure to comply with the New Reforms;
- claims for breach of fiduciary duty based on a new, more aggressive interpretation of the 'good faith' obligation.

While it is premature to predict the precise doctrinal contours that courts will follow, let alone how such claims will turn out, we can formulate the rationale the plaintiffs' bar will most likely develop for these claims and that they will be brought in state courts (primarily in Delaware courts, where over 50 per cent of the Fortune 500 companies

---

11 See *Telxon Corp.* v. *Meyerson*, 802 A.2d 257 (Del. 7 June 2002) (reversing grant of summary judgment); *Saito* v. *McKesson HBOC, Inc.*, 806 A.2d 113 (Del. 11 June 2002) (reversing decision limiting access to corporate books and records by shareholder investigating alleged wrongdoing); *Levco Alternative Fund Ltd.* v. *Reader's Digest Ass'n, Inc.*, 2002 WL 1859064 (Del. 13 Aug. 2002) (reversing denial of motion for preliminary injunction); *OmniCare, Inc.* v. *NCS Healthcare, Inc.*, 2002 WL 31767892 (Del. 10 Dec. 2002) (reversing denial of preliminary injunction); *MM Cos.* v. *Liquid Audio, Inc.*, No. 606, 2002 (Del. 7 January 2003) (reversing final judgment dismissing challenge to board decision to adopt defensive measures that changed the size and composition of the board during a proxy contest). See also *Gotham Partners, L.P.* v. *Hallwood Realty Partners, L.P.*, 2002 WL 31303135 (Del. 29 Aug. 2002) (affirming Court of Chancery's finding that general partner of a limited partnership breached its fiduciary duty to limited partners).

12 'What's Wrong with Executive Compensation? A Roundtable Moderated By Charles Elson', *Harvard Business Review* (January 2003), 68, 76.

and those listed on the NYSE are incorporated).[13] Indeed, two respected members of the Delaware judiciary, Chancellor William B. Chandler, III, and Vice Chancellor Leo E. Strine, Jr, recently co-authored an essay that discusses the likelihood that these types of new claims will emerge in state courts.[14]

The New Reforms address boardroom practices traditionally governed by state law principles and 'best practice' standards that have been advocated for years.[15] Undoubtedly, they will influence the corporation laws of all states, including Delaware, because of the inevitable conflict between the various state and federal laws and the rules imposed by the Exchanges.[16] But to what extent, if any, they usurp or pre-empt state corporation laws that govern the internal affairs of corporations, such as Delaware's, remains to be seen.[17] We predict that the state courts – namely Delaware courts – will be the first to hear cases based on requirements of the New Reforms.[18] Court adjudication of these issues will probably determine whether the state legislatures embrace or reject these requirements for their own corporation laws.

Why will the state courts, as opposed to the federal, be the first to hear cases involving the reforms? The most plausible answer is that

---

13 This is all in addition to federal enforcement actions by the SEC and federal criminal authorities, as well as proceedings initiated by the Exchanges to penalize companies that do not comply with the new reporting standards imposed by the 2002 Reforms and directed at preventing deception that harms the investor.

14 See William B. Chandler, III, and Leo E. Strine, Jr, 'The New Federalism Of The American Corporate Governance System: Preliminary Reflections of Two Residents of one Small State' (6 Jan. 2002), prepared for Penn Law and Economics Institute Conference on Control Transactions, 8–9 Feb. 2003 (draft), available at http://papers.ssrn.com/abstract=367720, at 37–44.

15 See, e.g., E. Norman Veasey, 'Delaware Corporation Law Ethics and Federalism', *The Metropolitan Corporate Counsel*, November 2002, 1; Ira M. Millstein and Paul W. MacAvoy, 'The Active Board of Directors and Performance of the Large Publicly Traded Corporation', *Columbia Law Review*, 98 (1998), 1,283; Chandler and Strine, 'The New Federalism', 4–5.

16 See Chandler and Strine, op. cit., 43–4.

17 See E. Norman Veasey, 'State–Federal Tension in Corporate Governance and the Professional Responsibilities of Advisors', 20 Feb. 2003, 5–7; E. Norman Veasey, 'Musings on the Dynamics of Corporate Governance Issues, Director Liability Concerns, Corporate Control Transactions, Ethics and Federalism' (8 Feb. 2003), 20–3; E. Norman Veasey, 'Reflections on Key Issues of the Professional Responsibilities of Corporate Lawyers in the Twenty-First Century' (28 October 2002), 3.

18 See Chandler and Strine, 'The New Federalism', 41–4.

Congress and the Exchanges failed to supply the means for the resolution of disputes by stockholders concerning implementation of the
reforms.[19] By act of Congress, the provisions of Sarbanes–Oxley are to
be enforced almost exclusively by the SEC or federal criminal authorities. There is no new private right of action for investors created by
Sarbanes–Oxley.[20]

Moreover, in the past, the federal courts generally have denied stockholders the right to enforce the rules of the Exchanges by means of
a private cause of action.[21] Finally, the Exchanges' chief enforcement
mechanism – the threat of de-listing or suspension of trading – is not an
appealing option to stockholders, as complainants, given that it leaves
them worse off than before de-listing.[22] These factors, in addition to the
stockholders' historical reluctance to rely entirely on the SEC and the
Exchanges to enforce federal law and regulations, indicate that state
courts will adjudicate a good many of the disputes arising out of the
reforms.[23]

As set forth by Chancellor Chandler and Vice Chancellor Strine – two
leading jurists who will be adjudicating these claims – there are various
forms in which the new state litigation could take shape. For instance,
plaintiffs may bring claims that allege the directors are breaching their
fiduciary duties by not complying with the new reforms.[24] In so doing,
shareholders may take a direct approach, arguing that Delaware's common law ought to embrace the substance of the new reforms (e.g., their
definition of 'independent director' or their requirement for independent approval of certain transactions).[25] Or shareholders simply could
argue that the directors breached their fiduciary duties by exposing the

---

19  See Chandler and Strine, 'The New Federalism', 38–41.
20  See Chandler and Strine, 'The New Federalism', 40 and n. 74 (citing Sarbanes–
    Oxley Act at § 3(b)(1) and Patricia A. Vlahakis *et al.*, *Corporate Governance
    Reform* (September/October 2002), 16. But see Sarbanes–Oxley § 306B
    (permitting private right of action to recover profits improperly obtained by
    insiders during pension fund black out periods) and, e.g., Sarbanes–Oxley
    § 302 (requiring that a company's periodic reports include certain certifications
    by the CEO and CFO, which could provide the basis of a private action).
21  See Chandler and Strine, 'The New Federalism', 39 and n. 73 (citing *Walck* v.
    *Am. Stock Exchange, Inc.*, 687 F.2d 778, 786 (3d Cir. 1982)).
22  See Chandler and Strine, 'The New Federalism', 38–9.
23  See Chandler and Strine, 'The New Fedralism', 40 and n. 75 ('active corporate
    plaintiffs' bar will be creative and aggressive in deploying the Reforms itself
    as a tool in shareholder litigation under state law').
24  See Chandler and Strine, 'The New Federalism', 42.
25  See Chandler and Strine, 'The New Federalism', 43.

corporation to an injurious sanction – such as de-listing – that may be imposed if the company does not conform to the reforms.[26] Further, there is the possibility that shareholders will seek injunctive relief to ensure that directors do not allow companies to violate the listing standards imposed by the Exchanges, and therefore, guarantee continued listing of the company's shares.[27]

The inevitable consequence of these new claims is that state courts may be compelled to determine whether directors have a fiduciary duty to ensure implementation of, and compliance with, the New Reforms. At this early stage, it is difficult to assess the outcome; however, directors that test the limits of state law by disregarding or acting carelessly with respect to the obligations imposed by the New Reforms could find themselves in trouble. Thus, directors and their advisers must at least take initial steps to strengthen procedures to comply with the heightened judicial scrutiny that is to come or be here liable for damages by their shareholders.[28]

Standards of conduct of directors are at the centre of this issue. It remains to be seen how far the courts will go to test them. According to Chief Justice E. Norman Veasey of the Delaware Supreme Court, '[s]tandards of conduct are the aspirational standards that directors should follow in carrying out their responsibilities to manage or direct the management of the business and affairs of the Corporation'.[29] Traditionally, as we have shown in Chapter 3, fiduciary duties have required directors to act with loyalty, due care, good faith, and the honest belief that they are acting in the best interests of the corporation:[30] that is, the director's motivation must be driven by the best

---

26　See Chandler and Strine, 'The New Federalism', 43.

27　See Chandler and Strine, 'The New Federalism', 43.

28　In addition, executive officers who are not directors should be aware that Chandler and Strine advocate amendments to Delaware's jurisdictional rules that would make it easier to hold key officers accountable for breach of fiduciary duty. See Chandler and Strine, 'The New Federalism', 65–6. According to Chandler and Strine, the Delaware courts have difficultly exercising personal jurisdiction over non-director officers whose conduct occurred outside Delaware: see ibid., 65–7. 'Given that the 2002 Reforms will increase the trend toward fewer management directors, it would make sense for Delaware to adopt a new subsection of [the Delaware director service statute] designed to cover top executives', so that stockholders could more easily hold 'these key corporate decision-makers accountable for failing to comply with their fiduciary duties': see ibid., 64–5.

29　Veasey, 'Musings', 8.

30　See ibid.

interests of the corporation and its stockholders and not by any personal, disloyal or bad faith interest.[31] The concepts of loyalty, care and good faith form the cornerstone of the business judgment rule, the presumption that business decisions made independently, with due care, and in good faith will not be overturned or even second guessed by the courts.[32]

However, one standard for director conduct that will be affected by the enhanced governance measures contained in the New Reform is the duty of good faith, which, according to the Chief Justice of the Delaware Supreme Court, 'is likely to emerge as a central issue of the directors' standard of conduct'.[33] The duty of good faith 'requires an honesty of purpose and eschews a disingenuous mindset of seeming to act for the corporate good, but not caring for the well being of the constituents of the fiduciary'.[34] Traditionally, the duty of good faith has been closely related to that of loyalty, which prohibits self-dealing, self-interest, or serving any interest except that of the corporation and its stockholders.[35] Chief Justice Veasey has noted, however, that, in some cases, it may be 'accurate to consider the duty of good faith as an additional duty beyond the duty of loyalty'.[36] According to Veasey, 'an argument could be made that reckless, irresponsible or irrational conduct – but not necessarily self-dealing or larcenous conduct – could implicate concepts of good faith'.[37] For example, 'the *utter failure* to follow the minimum expectations of Sarbanes–Oxley or the NYSE or NASDAQ Rules might likewise raise a good faith issue'.[38]

Chief Justice Veasey explains that that irrationality is the outer limit of the business judgment rule, and it may show that a decision is not made in good faith.[39] If a directors' decision is so beyond reason that no responsible assessment would credit it, then, according to Veasey, in some circumstances bad faith may be inferred.[40] Furthermore, Chief Justice Veasey states that corporations should 'genuinely and in good faith' have 'good corporate practices in place', and independent

---

31 See ibid.
32 See *Brehm* v. *Eisner*, 746 A.2d 244, 264, n.66 (Del. 2000).
33 See Veasey, 'Delaware Corporation Law', 13; Veasey, 'Musings', 6.
34 Veasey, 'Delaware Corporation Law', 12.
35 *Guth* v. *Loft*, 5 A.2d 503 (Del. 1939).
36 See Veasey, 'Delaware Corporation Law', 12.
37 See Veasey, ibid., 13.
38 See Veasey, ibid., 18 (emphasis in original); Veasey, 'State–Federal Tension', 13.
39 See Veasey, 'Delaware Corporation Law', 13; Veasey, 'Musings', 6.
40 See Veasey, 'Delaware Corporation Law', 13; Veasey, 'Musings', 6.

directors should 'have the guts to make sure those practices are followed, without being adversarial'.[41]

This declaration regarding the duty of good faith has implications for both the transmission of and the use of information in the corporation. Courts long have held that 'in making business decisions, directors must consider all material information reasonably available'.[42] The new set of expectations for director conduct created by Sarbanes–Oxley and the new listing requirements – as well as knowledge of the recent corporate failures – should play a role in court assessment with respect to whether material information that directors did not obtain nevertheless was reasonably available under proper governance procedures (that is, the courts could very well determine that directors *should* have known).

Under Delaware law, directors are fully protected from such a determination now when relying *in good faith* upon records, opinions, reports, and statements made by officers, employees, committees, or experts.[43] That is, such protection applies to directors dealing with issues within their professional competence who have been 'selected with reasonable care by or on behalf of the corporation'.[44] But what if the facts show that the directors' reliance was not sufficient, because the information provided was not all they should have had or, better yet, could have had with more effort and more independence from management sources? According to Chief Justice Veasey, 'the director may have fallen short of an expected standard of conduct',[45] which to us is to imply that such protection in those circumstances is no longer available.

A finding of liability based on lapses in the duty of good faith would be particularly significant in light of charter provisions of most corporations. These provisions have been modelled upon Section 102(b)(7) of the Delaware General Corporation Law, which permits shareholders to protect directors from liability for damages for breaches of the duty of care but not 'acts or omissions not in good faith'.[46] According to Chief Justice Veasey, the very language of Section 102(b)(7) 'seems to

---

41   *Harvard Business Review Roundtable*, 68, 76.
42   See, e.g., *Brehm* v. *Eisner*, 746 A.2d 244, 259 (Del. 2000); *Smith* v. *Van Gorkom*, 488 A.2d 858, 872–73 (Del. 1985); *Aronson* v. *Lewis*, 473 A.2d 805, 812 (Del. 1984).
43   See Veasey, 'Delaware Corporation Law', 14; Veasey, 'Musings', 7.
44   See Veasey, ibid., 14 (citing 8 Del. C. § 141(e); *Brehm*, 746 A.2d 261); Veasey, 'Musings', 7.
45   See Veasey, 'Delaware Corporation Law', 14; Veasey, 'Musings', 7.
46   8 Del. C. § 102(b)(7).

treat the duty of good faith as separate from the duty of care and the duty of loyalty', thus providing a basis for the theory that the two standards – good faith and loyalty – may be different in important respects.[47]

Considering the current environment of corporate scandals and the obligations imposed on directors by the New Reforms, we foresee that directors will face an increase in litigation. Lawsuits will go beyond traditional claims based on concepts of loyalty that allege self-dealing or self-interest by fiduciaries. Rather, the new and more challenging claims will allege breaches of good faith based on failures to embrace certain reform practices or ensure adequate access to information.

These claims will probably be most prevalent in connection with litigation against outside directors. Chief Justice Veasey has urged directors 'to demonstrate their independence, hold executive sessions, and follow governance procedures sincerely and effectively' in order to 'guard against anything that might happen to them in court'.[48] He further explains that '[d]irectors who are supposed to be independent should have the guts to be a pain in the neck and act independently'.[49] The implications of this statement obviously are open-ended.

The term 'outside director' refers to the first threshold in determining independence, which means a director is not a member of management. Under Delaware law, the term independence means 'that a director's decision is based on the corporate merits of the subject before the board rather than extraneous considerations or influences' that would 'convert an otherwise valid business decision into a faithless act'.[50] A director is not independent where he or she is beholden to or affiliated with an entity interested in the transaction 'or so under their influence that their discretion would be sterilized'.[51] To establish that a director 'does not maintain discretion to independently approve a transaction', a shareholder 'must demonstrate that the directors are 'beholden' [to a controlling shareholder or to management] because of personal or other relationships'.[52] Similarly, the term 'interestedness' relates to when a director will 'receive a personal financial benefit from

---

47  Veasey, 'Delaware Corporation Law', 16.
48  *Harvard Business Review Roundtable*, 76.
49  Ibid., 76.
50  *Aronson* v. *Lewis*, 473 A.2d 805, 816 (Del. 1984).
51  *Rales* v. *Blasband*, 634 A.2d 927, 936 (Del. 1993); see also *Grobow*, 539 A.2d 189; *Aronson*, 473 A.2d 815.
52  *Benerofe* v. *Cha*, 1996 WL 535405, at *7 (Del. Ch. 12 Sept. 1996), subsequent proceedings, 1998 WL 83081 (Del. Ch. 20 Feb. 1998).

a transaction that is not equally shared by the stockholders'.[53] Accordingly, the business judgment rule does not apply where 'directors have an interest other than as directors of the corporation'.[54]

The meaning – and possibly new meanings – of 'good faith' in light of the heightened expectations for directors take this concept of independence one step further. As Vice Chancellor Strine recently observed, corporate failures 'generate increased pressure on courts to examine carefully the plausibility of director claims that they were able to devote sufficient time to their duties to have carried them out in good faith'.[55] Vice Chancellor Strine notes that 'one can envision plaintiffs' lawyers who will try to take apart a board of directors based on the simple argument that the board simply could not have carried out its duties in the time devoted to them'.[56]

By way of example, plaintiffs pursuing arguments related to outside directors may ask courts to decide questions such as those listed below:

1 Could directors have had a good faith belief that they devoted enough board and/or committee time to oversight in light of the size and scope of the corporation's activities and – with 20/20 hindsight – what went wrong?
2 Could directors have had a good faith belief that an audit committee of a multi-billion dollar corporation that meets for two hours every quarter (and possibly with some members participating by phone) have devoted enough time and attention to oversight?
3 Could directors who have full time jobs and/or serve on multiple boards have had a good faith belief that their multiple obligations gave them enough time to exercise sufficient oversight over the affairs of each corporation they serve?
4 Could directors believe that their board can obtain all the information necessary to appropriately monitor management without a non-executive chairman?

Clearly, the issue that pervades these questions is the amount of time required for a director to satisfy his or her duty of oversight. Before the

---

53 *Rales*, 634 A.2d 936.
54 *Lewis* v. *S. L. & E., Inc.*, 629 F.2d 764, 769 (2d Cir. 1980).
55 Leo E. Strine, Jr., 'Derivative Impact? Some Early Reflections on the Corporation Law Implications of the Enron Debacle', *Business Lawyer*, 57 (2002), 1,371, 1,385.
56 Ibid., 1,386.

recent transgressions, it was widely recognized that proving liability for failure to monitor corporate affairs is 'possibly the most difficult theory in corporation law upon which a plaintiff might hope to win a judgment'.[57] But courts in the future will be presented with new challenges concerning this concept of limited director oversight duties, and will be asked to decide whether new common law rules should be created to impose greater risks of personal liability upon them. Some outside directors may increase their scrutiny of corporate affairs, while others may conclude that their directors' fees and other personal benefits are not worth the exposure to liability and stop serving on boards. We have heard anecdotal reports of directors stepping down and of difficulties some companies are having recruiting directors, but at this stage they are still cloakroom gossip. We are not currently convinced that a significant loss of directors is likely to occur. Indeed, the case could be made that directors on the verge of quitting because of increasing responsibility and liability are not the 'productive' directors and, by leaving, imply an average increase in the quality of boards.

Although the Delaware Supreme Court has not squarely so held, 'there may be potential personal liability, for the 'utter failure'... of the directors to assure that an adequate law compliance program is in place where that failure amounts to a sustained or systematic failure to exercise reasonable oversight, this potential finding however should be taken seriously'.[58] Recent federal appeals court decisions have reversed district court decisions dismissing claims challenging outside director oversight of corporate affairs in cases where shareholders had adopted Section 102(b)(7)-type charter provisions.[59] These courts reasoned that 'the duty of good faith may be breached where a director consciously disregards his duties to the corporation, thereby causing its stockholders to suffer'.[60] In light of the circumstances and facts in these cases, the courts held the 'magnitude and duration' of the problems were sufficient to create an issue of fact regarding the directors' good faith.[61] This goes beyond an adverse finding that the directors did not spend adequate time reviewing and deliberating on a specific transaction.

---

57  *In re Caremark Int'l Inc. Derivative Litig.*, 698 A.2d 959, 967 (Del. Ch. 1996).
58  See Veasey, 'Delaware Corporation Law', 18; Veasey, 'State–Federal Tension', 13.
59  See *McCall* v. *Scott*, 239 F.3d 808 (6th Cir.), modified, 250 F.3d 997 (6th Cir. 2001) (construing Delaware law).
60  *McCall*, 250 F.3d at 1001.
61  *McCall*, 239 F.3d at 823.

It also has been argued that the committees on which outside directors serve should employ new methods to strengthen oversight. Chief Justice Veasey recently expressed his opinion that compensation committees should have their own advisers and lawyers.[62] This proposal raises numerous basic questions: to what extent can compensation committees rely upon the corporation's advisers and lawyers? To what extent can other committees – such as audit committees, which under the Sarbanes–Oxley Act have 'authority to engage independent counsel and other advisors, as it determines necessary to carry out its duties' – rely upon the corporation's advisers and lawyers? Should the board as a whole have its own advisers and lawyers? Can the board and/or more than one committee utilize the same advisers and counsel? To what extent will a compensation or audit committee determination not to retain their own advisers and lawyers – based upon cost considerations and/or their confidence in the board's advisers – face allegations that the failure to do so reflected something less than good faith? Are all committees obliged to at least consider whether they need their own adviser and counsel? If so, can reliance upon the company's advisers and counsel on that subject possibly be deemed to reflect something less than good faith?

The courts will decide the extent to which outside directors face personal liability. It is our position that the judiciary's response to the director's new oversight responsibility should have an impact upon the way outside directors monitor corporate affairs and take responsibility for the results. We foresee that the judiciary will be confronted with the issue of independent board leadership in connection with the director's duty of good faith. As discussed, key members of the judiciary already have exhibited an increased awareness and sensitivity to the concept of good faith as it relates to directors' standard of conduct.[63] Indeed, as has been noted, Chief Justice Veasey has expressed the view that, in connection with the new standards mandated by voluntary best practices,

---

62  See *Harvard Business Review Roundtable*, 76.
63  See discussion above.

'good faith is likely to emerge as a central issue of the directors' standard of conduct'.[64] We agree.

## Recommendations

There are changes to be made in governance to help boards fulfil, and demonstrate their fulfilment of, their responsibilities to shareholders, including their duty of good faith. We believe corporations that carry out our recommendations, adapted to their own unique corporate circumstances, will have little to fear from enforcement by private plaintiffs or public complaints alleging failure by the management and the board of directors to carry out their responsibilities.

It is time to clear away the cobwebs that have clouded the description of board responsibilities. The boardroom is not meant to be a clubroom, or solely a collegial forum supportive of management, in which directors receive reports, ask pro forma questions, and depend on management for answers to questions critical of management agendas. Neither is it meant to be a body solely adversarial with management, in a continuous hunt for trouble, looking to depose management at the first sign of a performance slip.

The board is there to care for other people's money, that of the shareholders; its major responsibility is to them. That responsibility cannot easily be reduced to slogans, and surely it cannot be reduced to any one magic nostrum. That responsibility is most complex, and its exercise requires serious balancing: learning the business but not running it; nurturing and rewarding management but replacing it (early but not too early) when necessary; listening carefully to and respecting management proposals, but questioning management's premises and factual support so as to distinguish management self-interest from the corporate good; certifying strategic plans from management, but also proposing

---

64 Veasey, 'Delaware Corporation Law', 13. In fact, this is beginning to occur. Recently, the Delaware Court of Chancery rejected a motion to dismiss a shareholder derivative lawsuit, in part, on grounds that the facts, as alleged, could constitute a breach of the 'directors' obligation to act honestly and in good faith' (*In re The Walt Disney Co. Derivative Litig.*, Del. Ch., C.A. No. 15452, Chandler, C., Memorandum Opinion (May 28, 2003), 28). According to the Memorandum Opinion, the complaint alleged that 'the defendant directors *knew* that they were making material decisions without adequate information and without adequate deliberation', which, if proven, could constitute a breach of the directors' duty to act in good faith and lead to liability (ibid.: emphasis in original).

alternatives and participating in new strategy development; acting in a collegial manner but also in an adversarial manner when necessary; being willing to compromise when it is legitimate to do so; and not witch hunting, but sufficiently anticipating trouble so as to self-correct before the regulators and plaintiffs get there.

Board members must understand and live with balancing points of view and have the dedication and time to cope with diverse views and positions before making an informed judgement in good faith. They most of all must understand there is a real job to be done as fiduciaries for people they do not know and cannot see, but who count on their honesty, loyalty, diligence and good faith for protection.

The reform proposals we make are designed to enable the board to perform its complex role. Most imperative is the separation of the roles of chairman and CEO. We suggest additional initiatives to ensure that the board focuses on the right issues and is provided with complete and accurate information for all board assessments and decisions.

1  Boards should separate the roles of chairman and CEO and designate an independent director as chairman.
2  Boards should determine to their satisfaction that management has appropriate processes in place to prepare the certification required by the Sarbanes–Oxley Act.
3  Boards should take responsibility for the company's strategy, risk management, and financial reporting based on sufficient knowledge of the company's business environment, challenges, and opportunities, and should carefully construct compensation arrangements to reward extraordinary company (not market) performance.
4  Boards should assure themselves of the integrity of management.

Additional steps should be taken to meet board information needs, including the following:

1  Boards should structure their meetings so as to ensure that issues central to the performance of the company are given sufficient time, and that management presentations concerning such issues present options, and not simply reports.
2  Boards should assure themselves that board agendas prioritize and carry out the foregoing rules of practice.
3  To further their access to information beyond the requirements of the Sarbanes–Oxley Act the company's internal auditor should be hired by and report to the board.

4 Boards should feel free, without the consent of management, to retain such consultants and advisers as they deem necessary to carry out their responsibilities.

5 Boards should expand their definition of management and establish procedures for familiarizing themselves with business leaders below the level of senior management.

The likelihood that this programme of reform would be effective can be assessed by the strength of management opposition. In practice, we expect that most of our suggestions, other than separation of the chair and CEO roles, would be difficult to mandate by legislation, SEC regulation or listing requirements. How they would be carried out depends largely on the nature of each business, its volatility, its risks, challenges and opportunities, its reporting processes and other matters unique to the organization. Only within that context can a judgment be made as to how much board process is required, how much information is required, and how much incentive is required. These are matters for each board to decide, and for each board's independent chairman to implement.

Most fundamental, the effectiveness of a board's response to its unique situation should be the test by which its good faith in carrying out its responsibilities is measured.

It is incredible to us that there are boards today that are willing to risk not having the information they need to meet their responsibilities. Can there be any question that the information in real time on the product-by-product output and sales performance is essential to the board's ability to be the expected 'check' on management? How can directors go about obtaining the necessary information concerning the business, the strategy, the risks, the personnel, the potential failures in performance, reporting systems, and any number of other potential issues? This is a valid concern especially since the majority of directors typically come to the company just six or eight times a year, for a few hours each time, with an agenda set by the CEO, and information given to them under the watchful eye of the CEO whose performance they are supposed to be monitoring.

We cannot lay down hard and fast rules on how to obtain this information; it will be up to each board to devise its own system applying our reform principles to their respective business. Some boards have come to the realization that they do not have the information needed to function properly, and now are attempting to design processes to ensure that they get what they need when they need it. As we have shown, recent court decisions have provided a wake-up call. In order to monitor management effectively – and sufficiently, in light of emerging legal responsibilities – directors must know more, and understand more, about how the company functions.

The 'gatekeepers' – the lawyers, accountants, bankers – can assist the directors to obtain the information they require, but the board is where the buck stops. In our view, this is the central challenge of the new reforms – with the considerable responsibilities shifted back to the board (where they have always belonged), the board must identify and take control of its own agenda and information needs. To do so, the board needs to self-help; it needs to correct itself.

The major element of self-help, as suggested throughout this book, requires boards to own up and recognize the basic truth: a board needs a leader, separate and independent from management, whose primary function is to help the entire board design and carry out its processes and thereby obtain the information that it needs to adequately protect against the misuse of resources and the squandering of investor's capital.

The ideal board is comprised of many different types of people, with each individual director chosen with regard to the specific attributes, experience and expertise he or she offers the company. While the exact mix of personalities and experiences required depends on the needs of the company, 8, 10, or 16 men and women with different backgrounds and life experiences, as collegial as they may try to be, cannot, in our view, meet the new challenges and responsibilities of the board without someone assuming leadership. Directors are corporate outsiders, with other careers and responsibilities. Individually they typically lack the time and resources needed to obtain the requisite inside knowledge to perform their significant monitoring role. One member of the board, independent of the CEO, must have the primary responsibility of, and devote the time necessary to, getting the other directors informed, by helping them focus on the issues that are important to the shareholders, and on the risks facing the corporation. Coordination, integration, communication, and moulding a group of disparate individuals into a mutually supportive team working to foster management's success does not happen magically. It requires leadership. In our view, the need for the function of leadership in the boardroom is undeniable.

In his recent book *Corporate Governance and Chairmanship*, Sir Adrian Cadbury adds another element of the chairman's role. He writes that the 'key quality' of the separate chairman is 'that required of a good coach ... [whose] satisfaction derives from the achievements of those they coach ... The role of the chairmen is to support their chief executives, and to enjoy their success and whatever reflected glory goes with it.'[65] Effective chairmen are concerned with the effectiveness of their board as a whole and their task is to provide whatever form of leadership is needed to bring out the best in their board teams at any given time. Because board members and challenges to the corporation change, 'the role of [the] chairman does not remain fixed'.[66] Given the time and experience that leading a board requires, assigning the task of board leadership to the CEO almost inevitably means that the quality of board leadership will suffer. Leading the board today is a job; it is not an honorary position. It is difficult to imagine how one person, in a complex business, can do both jobs – leading the board and CEO-ing the business – without one of those important jobs being neglected.

The chairman should be the CEO's coach and confidant. He or she should be involved in setting the board agenda, and managing the flow of information to the board. He or she should facilitate communication among directors; integrate the activities of the board committees; and, with the board's understanding, communicate needed messages between the board and the CEO. The chairman should meld the board into a cohesive group of men and women who, although they may often hold differences of opinion, are unified in supporting and fostering the success of their CEO. The chairman should do all of this, while bringing the board to believe truly that each director, including the chairman, is equal, and free to communicate directly with management.

If this step is not taken we believe that the failure to have independent board leadership might, in the new world of judicial review, give rise to challenges in connection with directors' duty of good faith. And to repeat, by independent board leadership we mean more than the part time lead director who sits in the chairman' seat during executive sessions as required by the stock exchange proposals. We mean a full time chairman who is not the CEO.

Additionally, separating the role of CEO and chairman is conceptually the right thing to do if one believes that checks and balances – and reigning-in unfettered power – apply in governance as they do in government. A board needs leadership separate from the CEO, to serve as a check on management, to respond to expanded demands for

---

65 Adrian Cadbury, *Corporate Governance and Chairmanship'* (Oxford University Press, 2002), 177–8.
66 Ibid., 103.

accountability and transparency reflected in the Sarbanes–Oxley Act and proposed listing rules and, more importantly, to help the board implement the additional self-help recommendations we have set forth above. A separate chairman would lead the board and assist it in managing its responsibilities, while allowing the CEO to focus on managing the business.

How, practically, is that to be accomplished? Notwithstanding our central argument that the chairman and CEO be separate, we recognize the need to be pragmatic. The board cannot simply strip the title from a sitting chairman/CEO and hand it to someone else. Removing a title from such an individual looks like a demotion and sends a message that the board lacks confidence in the corporation's leadership. Instead, boards should view separation as a key issue to be resolved in succession, to be implemented when whoever is serving in both roles steps down. Our experience is that the lead director works for the chairman, with the result that complexities are increased and the inherent conflicts in the executive chairmanship are not resolved. While the appointment of a 'lead' or 'presiding' director, may be the beginning of the process, as we have stated, it is not enough. Thus, while the institutionalization of a lead director may be better than nothing, a concerted effort should be made to institutionalize the concept of an independent chairman. In fact, the exchanges need not even mandate that different individuals fill the two jobs, but their listing requirements should require that a listed company either separate the roles of CEO and chairman or explain why it has not done so. The separate chairman can be anyone, from a person who once fulfilled both roles to a new and independent outsider. There is flexibility: it is up to each board to determine what will work best and to explain its determination to the shareholders.

Recently, the UK government commissioned Derek Higgs to lead a review of the role and effectiveness of non-executive directors in the UK. The report was issued in January 2003 and contains a concise and quite adaptable summary of the role of the chairman:

The Chairman is responsible for:

- leadership of the board, ensuring its effectiveness on all aspects of its role and setting its agenda;
- ensuring the provision of accurate, timely and clear information to directors;
- ensuring effective communication with shareholders;

- arranging the regular evaluation of the performance of the board, its committees and individual directors, and
- facilitating the effective contribution of non-executive directors and ensuring constructive relations between executive and non-executive directors.'[67]

There are important differences in governance structure between the UK and the USA, but these general principles will certainly be useful to corporations in either country seeking, in good faith, to develop their own separation arrangements. One principle, however, is essential: whatever the separation arrangement, it should be defined clearly so as to avoid ambiguity as to the roles.

There is, as expected, opposition from sitting CEOs to separating the titles. As articulated, the argument is that 'two people cannot run the company'. But we do not suggest that; the CEO will manage the company, and the chairman will lead the board's activities. We suspect the opposition is more a basic resistance to the shift of additional power and responsibility to the board, as envisioned by the Sarbanes–Oxley Act, the new listing requirements, and vital reform proposals such as ours.

That is, then, the message from a lawyer and an economist, both duly seasoned by many board experiences in many circumstances. Fix the board. It is not that difficult, if everyone gives in a little and honestly considers what a board needs to perform as it should. The board cannot function without leadership separate from the management it is supposed to monitor. On behalf of the shareholders, the board must be enabled to obtain the information necessary to monitor, in good faith, the performance of management in all respects. It has a responsibility to do so. Now it must be empowered with the opportunity to fulfill this responsibility.

Perhaps with these reforms, the recurring crises in governance will take place with less frequency and intensity.

---

67  Derek Higgs, *Review of the Role and Effectiveness of Non-Executive Directors*, 20 January 2003, 23.

# Appendix A: Technical Implementation Issues in the Analysis of EVA™ for CalPERS-rated Companies

This Appendix provides greater detail concerning two problems we faced in generating results on the relation of EVA™ to CalPERS ratings as reported in Chapter 5. Creating a sample of consistent data posed significant problems, and inferences and assumptions were frequently made during calculations that merit evaluations here.

## Sample determination

Of the 300 companies selected by CalPERS for its survey, a significant number had to be eliminated from this study because of data deficiencies. There were 76 firms excluded because they did not respond to the CalPERS request. In addition, financial service and holding companies were excluded since they frequently exhibit near-zero or negative operating capital, resulting in asymptotically high or low values for returns on invested capital. Financial institutions generate low or negative operating capital, in part because of the assumption of conservatism inherent in most accounting valuations of assets. This condition, coupled with the size of assets and liabilities relative to earnings, and the fluctuations in assets and liabilities, led to negative rates of return even when earnings were positive (implying a negative invested capital stock) or to earnings exceeding capital to a factor of ten (when capital is positive, but near zero). A particularly egregious example is Citicorp. The data in Table A.1 display the two critical components of ROIC – NOPLAT and OIC – for the period 1991–95, in millions of dollars.

Holding companies, such as Berkshire Hathaway or American Brands (now Fortune Brands), demonstrated similar behaviour, taking in invested capital and acquiring shares in other companies. When these acquisitions were made at a value greater than the accounting book value, the difference was represented as 'goodwill', and was not included as an asset for the purposes of this study. Thus,

*Table A.1*  Example estimation of rates of return (Citicorp)

|  | 1991 | 1992 | 1993 | 1994 | 1995 |
|---|---|---|---|---|---|
| ROIC | 13.9% | 28.3% | 108.5% | 1,075.7% | −17.0% |
| NOPLAT | $2,702 | $3,050 | $3,634 | $5,228 | $2,915 |
| OIC | $19,508 | $10,795 | $3,349 | $486 | −$17,181 |

if goodwill is excluded, under this model the normal operation of holding companies will lead them to create negative OIC. One holding company (Unicom) was primarily a holding company for another firm already in the study (Commonwealth Edison) and was removed. Eliminating financial institutions and holding companies took 39 companies out of the CalPERS sample.

Two more companies, NBD Bancorp and Shawmut, were excluded from the CalPERS grading system because both were undergoing reorganization during the course of the survey.

One further company, Roadway Services, was a new issue in 1994 and therefore did not exist long enough to generate sufficient data to calculate WACC figures for 1995.

Merger activity has posed serious problems for the spread calculation upon which this study was based. The ROIC calculation uses the operating invested capital figures from the beginning of a given year and compares them with earnings at year-end, so that merger activity in the middle of the year can skew the results of ROIC calculations. An extreme example of this phenomenon can be found in Columbia/HCA, which merged during 1993 (see Table A.2; all figures in millions of dollars) as can be the merger boosted sales and earnings during 1993, but OIC was not affected until 1994. For this study the purpose of ROIC calculations is to simulate the investment decision of a prospective investor who, when evaluating firms at the beginning of a year, applies the then-current WACC to valuation models. At the end of the year, the investor can then examine the results of that investment. To counteract this effect, data for years and firm combinations where companies may have engaged in extensive merger activity were examined. Aside from Columbia/HCA, the other two primary instances of merger conduct concerning companies that were included in the database are Burlington Northern in 1993 and the merger of Lockheed and Martin Marietta in 1994. The Columbia/HCA was eventually excluded from the database altogether as COMPUSTAT™ did not have adequate financial data for the ten-year period under review. Burlington Northern's entry for 1993 was removed from the database.

A special case is the Lockheed Martin merger of 1994. Two complications arise from the fact that the two merging entities were previously in the database. The first is how to define and measure the different entities during the 1991–95 period. The solution was to include an entry for Lockheed for 1991–93 and to append Lockheed Martin data to Lockheed during 1994–95. The valuation for the critical merger year of 1994 uses the combined OIC for Lockheed and Martin at the beginning of 1994.

*Table A.2*   Example estimation of income (Columbia/HCA)

|  | *1992* | *1993* | *1994* |
| --- | --- | --- | --- |
| Net sales (year end) | $807 | $10,252 | $11,132 |
| Earning before income taxes (year end) | $86 | $1,434 | $1,605 |
| Operating investing capital (year end) | $377 | $849 | $5,851 |

Another 26 companies have been removed from the sample due to bankruptcy and/or acquisition by another company in the later 1990s. We also chose to remove American Home Products for 2001 as an unusual and substantial increase in non-interest bearing liabilities that year resulted in an artificially low OIC. Finally, 26 firms were removed from the sample because they were regulated utilities for which 'spread' was controlled by regulatory practices, without regard for governance systems. A full listing of each company in the study and its status is on file with the authors.

## WACC estimation procedures

Generating a full set of numbers for ROIC and WACC required creating a standardized set of financial statistics for a series of firms that had inconsistent and incomplete data. ROIC calculations were generally straightforward; WACC calculations, on the other hand, required multiple procedures of defining the cost and amount of debt and equity. These different methods are described in succeeding paragraphs.

As noted earlier, cost of debt is defined as follows:

Interest Cost * (1 – Tax Rate)

Interest cost is represented by the first number that can be derived from the following hierarchy.

1   Interest expense.
2   Book Value of Debt (where available) * Interest Rate (based on appropriate Standard & Poor's (S&P) bond rating from the December Industrial Index).[1]
3   The Federal tax rate is assumed to be a flat rate of 35 per cent. Additional state taxes of 5 per cent are assumed, bringing the rate to 40 per cent.
4   Cost of preferred stock is represented as preferred stock dividends.

Total cost of common equity, as discussed earlier, is represented as follows:

Equity Cost = Beta $(R_M - R_F) + R_F$

Each of the variables in this identity needs to be defined. Beta is represented in COMPUSTAT™ as a regression of monthly stock and S&P 500 values over a period of up to five years, if data permit, but for no less then three years. For many newer companies, there were not sufficient months to generate beta values for the entire sample period. In these cases, betas for these years were substituted by the lifetime average betas for the company taken for the available years. The return on the market $(R_M)$ is represented by the compound return on large-company stocks for the preceding ten-year period as reported by Ibbotson Associates.[2] The risk-free return is the compounded US Treasury bill rate for the calendar year,

---

1   See *Standard and Poor's Bond Guide 3*, edited by Frank L.Vaglio (1996).
2   See Ibbotson Associates, *Stocks, Bonds, Bills and Inflation 2002 Yearbook*, 298–299 Table C-1 (2002).

as generated by Ibbotson and Associates.[3] The equity number is the market value of common stock taken from the COMPUSTAT™ database.

## Complete regression results

The complete set of included variables and coefficients is reported in Table A.3. We conclude that there is a significant variation in annual as well as industry performance; the control for these variations is by inclusion of relevant year

*Table A.3* Regression for single company annual value added versus CalPERS grades

|  | Coefficient | Standard error | t-value |
|---|---|---|---|
| Constant | −12.192** | 3.600 | −3.39 |
| 1991 | −1.341 | 2.710 | −0.49 |
| 1993 | 3.878 | 2.710 | 1.43 |
| 1994 | 7.196** | 2.705 | 2.66 |
| 1995 | 9.407** | 2.705 | 3.48 |
| 1996 | 8.715** | 2.705 | 3.22 |
| 1997 | 5.650** | 2.705 | 2.09 |
| 1998 | 4.352 | 2.716 | 1.60 |
| 1999 | 8.957** | 2.750 | 3.26 |
| 2000 | 7.933** | 2.781 | 2.85 |
| 2001 | 11.948** | 2.808 | 4.26 |
| Aerospace | 11.553** | 4.410 | 2.62 |
| Automotive | 9.258** | 4.227 | 2.19 |
| Chemicals | 8.966** | 3.706 | 2.42 |
| Computers | 14.885** | 3.630 | 4.10 |
| Electrical equipment | 18.568** | 7.203 | 2.58 |
| Foods | 19.402** | 4.410 | 4.40 |
| Health care | 22.258** | 3.514 | 6.33 |
| Machinery | 13.692** | 3.779 | 3.62 |
| Miscellaneous | 10.030** | 3.422 | 2.93 |
| Oil/gas | 4.980 | 3.350 | 1.49 |
| Retail | 20.701** | 3.214 | 6.44 |
| Telecom equipment | −4.886 | 5.562 | −0.88 |
| Transportation | 6.180 | 3.987 | 1.55 |
| CalPERS Grade A, B | −3.381** | 1.423 | −2.38 |
| CalPERS Grade C, D, F | −2.746 | 1.515 | −1.81 |
| $R^2$ (adj) (%) | 11.1 | | |

*Note*: Sample size = 128. All figures are percentages. Statistically significant coefficients at 5 per cent level are denoted by **.

3 See ibid.

variables. The years of the Clinton Administration show significantly higher performance than the early years of the 1990s. Companies in the computer, health care, food and retail industries demonstrate superior performance. The regression accounts for 11 per cent of the variation in economic value added, which we consider to be high given the low level of precision of the explanatory variables.

## Econometric issues

Here we briefly discuss econometric issues that we had to deal with, and describe the solutions that we found to be appropriate.

The main sample used in the study consists of 128 companies, with 11 annual observations per company for almost all companies. That corresponds to a total of 1,366 observations for the dependant variable. Therefore, the number of explanatory variables used in this regression, 22, is adequate. The effects of business cycle variation on economic returns has been accounted for by including annual binary variables, with industry variation accounted for by addition of industry dummies. We take the position that the residual effect of active versus passive corporate governance on economic performance of the company is measured by regressing performance on CalPERS grade for governance. The F-statistic provides a measure of joint statistical significance of all included explanatory variables. The statistic indicates that the variables are extremely important, with $F_{(25,1340)} - 7.84$ when the ninety-ninth percentile is at 2.17. The regressors explain 11 per cent of the variance.

In the regression analysis of board change and its effect on economic performance, we encountered multicollinearity. The board change variable is correlated with year dummies, since most of the changes took place in the middle of the observation period. A standard solution to this problem is to exclude a subset of the variables; however, we did not want to exclude annual variations, for then we would not be able to distinguish the effects of the business cycle and board change on performance. The compromise was to substitute annual dummies with variables related to the year of the board change.

Due to the smaller sample size (29 companies, with 11 observations per company), we also decided to combine industries into larger segments or sectors, based on our perception of production functions and other similarities. The F-statistic for these regressions are $F_{(8,223)} - 7.44$ and $F_{(6,225)}$ with the ninety-ninth percentile being at 4.86 and 6.88. The regressions explain 18.2 to 18.5 per cent of the variance.

# Appendix B: Database of EVA™ Estimates

The observations listed here are estimates for EVA™ from recent COMPUSTAT™ data up to 2001. These estimates are based on the official financial statements of each of the companies rated by CalPERS for governance efficacy used in the analytical studies in Chapters 5 and 6.

Table B.1  Database of EVA™ Estimates (per cent)

| Company name | CalPERS grade | 1991 | 1992 | 1993 | 1994 | 1995 | 1996 | 1997 | 1998 | 1999 | 2000 | 2001 |
|---|---|---|---|---|---|---|---|---|---|---|---|---|
| Alcan Aluminium | A+ | -11.9 | -11.4 | -10.5 | -9.8 | -4.4 | -6.5 | -9.9 | -16.63 | -14.0 | -4.9 | -9.1 |
| Amoco Corp. | A+ | -8.7 | -8.5 | 0.8 | -1.3 | -2.1 | 0.5 | -1.0 | -20.21 | | | |
| Amp Inc. | A+ | -8.0 | -2.6 | -0.8 | 3.8 | 4.3 | 2.7 | -4.1 | -4.82 | | | |
| Amr Corp./De | A+ | -14.0 | -16.6 | -7.4 | -4.2 | -2.0 | 3.9 | 2.3 | 1.29 | -7.8 | -0.3 | -22.0 |
| Ashland Inc. | A+ | -3.3 | -18.6 | -1.1 | -2.1 | -5.3 | -3.6 | -7.7 | -9.56 | 11.2 | 6.4 | 6.3 |
| Avon Products | A+ | 7.4 | 15.4 | 25.4 | 34.7 | 33.3 | 37.4 | 25.8 | 21.84 | 19.5 | 36.9 | 27.2 |
| Bristol Myers SQ | A+ | 14.4 | 6.7 | 10.8 | 17.9 | 23.8 | 28.3 | 34.6 | 27.43 | 37.8 | 34.9 | 36.9 |
| Campbell Soup Co. | A+ | 4.4 | 5.4 | -3.0 | 16.5 | 16.2 | 21.7 | 20.4 | 26.10 | 37.2 | 38.5 | 43.0 |
| Caterpillar Inc. | A+ | -9.6 | -13.0 | 4.9 | 10.9 | 13.8 | 13.6 | 14.7 | 10.08 | 1.8 | 3.6 | 2.9 |
| Chevron Corp. | A+ | -8.5 | -3.9 | -3.2 | -6.7 | -9.8 | 0.6 | 4.7 | -3.33 | 2.2 | 3.5 | 14.9 |
| Cisco Systems Inc. | A+ | 32.7 | 36.5 | 53.1 | 102.0 | 74.7 | 64.8 | 30.7 | 22.76 | 29.7 | 70.9 | -42.8 |
| Colgate-Palmolive | A+ | -2.6 | 5.9 | 14.0 | 19.1 | 8.8 | 17.7 | 10.8 | 16.50 | 8.5 | 19.7 | 33.6 |
| Cooper Industries | A+ | 0.8 | -16.8 | 1.4 | 0.8 | 5.9 | 22.7 | 22.6 | 10.64 | 25.0 | 26.9 | 18.1 |
| Dayton Hudson Corp. | A+ | -6.6 | -0.7 | -0.5 | 4.4 | 0.4 | 2.2 | -2.0 | -6.29 | -6.4 | -3.6 | 2.0 |
| Deere & Co. | A+ | -7.1 | -4.8 | -0.7 | 3.2 | 3.9 | 0.7 | 1.9 | -2.19 | -6.0 | -1.4 | -2.7 |
| Delta Air Lines Inc. | A+ | -28.0 | -28.9 | -24.4 | -11.9 | -2.5 | 3.5 | 12.1 | 18.12 | 19.2 | 10.9 | -25.7 |
| Deluxe Corp. | A+ | 16.5 | 15.2 | 12.4 | 6.8 | 4.9 | 11.4 | 18.6 | 21.35 | 17.8 | 20.0 | 49.7 |
| Exxon Corp. | A+ | -3.1 | -3.5 | -0.2 | -3.4 | -1.0 | -0.7 | 0.3 | -4.38 | 5.6 | 7.5 | 8.6 |
| Gap Inc. | A+ | 21.4 | 11.1 | 10.9 | 9.4 | 8.2 | 12.6 | 18.6 | 19.51 | 28.7 | 9.0 | -15.9 |
| General Motors | A+ | -6.7 | -4.7 | 0.1 | 3.8 | 2.6 | -0.3 | -0.5 | -0.96 | -1.1 | -2.5 | -3.5 |
| Hershey Foods Corp. | A+ | 2.7 | 0.8 | -4.6 | 2.6 | 3.0 | 10.9 | 15.0 | 20.01 | 12.7 | 14.9 | 18.0 |
| Hewlett-Packard Co. | A+ | -9.0 | -16.2 | -10.4 | -7.1 | 2.1 | -3.0 | -8.7 | -11.13 | -7.8 | -7.8 | -11.0 |
| Illinois Tool Works | A+ | -2.1 | 9.2 | 14.1 | 7.7 | 6.0 | 13.0 | 11.3 | 13.43 | 25.3 | 15.2 | 6.9 |
| Ingersoll-Rand Co. | A+ | -11.1 | -20.8 | -6.1 | 3.3 | 3.8 | 8.6 | 1.8 | 21.82 | 25.1 | 19.0 | 16.0 |

Table B.1 Continued

| Company name | CalPERS grade | 1991 | 1992 | 1993 | 1994 | 1995 | 1996 | 1997 | 1998 | 1999 | 2000 | 2001 |
|---|---|---|---|---|---|---|---|---|---|---|---|---|
| IBM Corp. | A+ | -12.2 | -5.6 | -10.7 | -3.6 | -0.8 | -1.1 | -6.9 | -5.79 | -3.6 | -1.8 | -1.4 |
| Intl Paper Co. | A+ | -9.3 | -1.2 | -2.4 | -3.3 | 4.5 | 0.0 | -11.1 | -8.69 | -6.3 | 0.5 | -9.5 |
| Jostens Inc. | A+ | 8.5 | 3.2 | -10.1 | -8.8 | 0.9 | 0.8 | 16.9 | 24.95 | 28.8 | | |
| K-Mart Corp. | A+ | -4.0 | -9.1 | -13.3 | -3.8 | -9.9 | -4.5 | -3.2 | -5.11 | -5.4 | -10.2 | -26.9 |
| Kimberly-Clark | A+ | -1.4 | -2.5 | 1.7 | 0.4 | 7.7 | 5.8 | 4.1 | 6.01 | 10.5 | 13.7 | 16.6 |
| Lockheed Martin | A+ | -1.0 | 4.0 | 12.4 | 26.7 | 10.7 | 16.7 | 11.9 | 15.36 | 10.6 | 3.0 | 16.3 |
| Lowes Cos | A+ | -15.0 | -13.5 | -8.6 | 0.2 | 6.2 | 4.6 | 1.7 | -0.29 | -1.1 | -6.8 | -1.8 |
| McDonalds Corp. | A+ | -2.0 | 0.6 | 0.7 | -0.3 | -1.4 | 2.2 | -0.3 | -3.14 | -0.2 | -0.9 | 5.5 |
| McKesson Corp. | A+ | -5.8 | 5.4 | 8.2 | -18.0 | -6.5 | -8.3 | 0.6 | -4.29 | -4.7 | -2.6 | 10.3 |
| Merck & Co. | A+ | 29.5 | 19.9 | 33.8 | 41.5 | 24.9 | 19.2 | 29.0 | 35.16 | 34.6 | 48.1 | 44.0 |
| Mobil Corp. | A+ | -7.5 | -7.2 | -3.4 | -3.8 | -5.7 | 1.3 | -1.5 | -7.85 | | | |
| Northern Telecom | A+ | 2.8 | -1.4 | -13.9 | -3.0 | -3.2 | -4.9 | -4.0 | -17.46 | -20.0 | -37.4 | -73.3 |
| Penney (J C) Co. | A+ | -9.5 | -0.7 | 2.5 | 5.3 | 0.4 | 0.1 | -1.6 | -2.06 | -4.0 | -10.9 | -1.5 |
| Pfizer Inc. | A+ | -4.2 | -14.9 | -5.9 | 9.2 | 9.3 | 8.5 | 6.1 | 5.63 | 15.5 | 27.6 | 34.5 |
| Philip Morris Cos Inc. | A+ | 25.4 | 35.7 | 19.3 | 40.0 | 49.9 | 60.9 | 63.5 | 63.08 | 57.2 | 74.3 | 129.9 |
| Phillips Petroleum | A+ | -14.8 | -10.3 | -9.5 | -5.3 | -3.8 | 3.7 | 2.1 | -7.81 | -0.7 | 11.6 | 20.5 |
| PPG Industries Inc. | A+ | -8.8 | -3.4 | -5.5 | 6.6 | 7.8 | 6.0 | 3.6 | 4.47 | 2.7 | 3.3 | 3.4 |
| Readers Digest Assn | A+ | 37.9 | 32.2 | 36.8 | 42.4 | 60.4 | 47.6 | 31.2 | 0.98 | 30.5 | 24.2 | 591.1 |
| Rockwell Intl Corp. | A+ | -2.8 | -14.4 | 9.3 | 9.1 | 10.3 | -0.5 | 1.0 | -9.81 | 2.9 | 3.3 | -0.4 |
| Rohm & Haas Co. | A+ | -7.2 | -11.0 | -4.0 | 3.7 | 3.8 | 4.2 | -4.9 | -0.68 | 49.0 | -7.9 | -5.2 |
| Schlumberger Ltd. | A+ | 0.8 | -3.6 | -2.7 | -0.9 | -0.2 | 6.4 | 6.1 | -1.56 | -12.1 | -7.6 | -4.9 |
| Sherwin-Williams Co. | A+ | -3.6 | -14.2 | 0.3 | 1.7 | 7.2 | 9.0 | 11.1 | 7.66 | 8.1 | 5.3 | 15.0 |
| Sonat Inc. | A+ | -9.4 | -3.4 | -2.2 | -0.7 | -3.0 | 1.2 | 2.9 | -10.5 | | | |
| Texas Instruments | A+ | -32.0 | -6.9 | -0.9 | 6.7 | 13.3 | -24.4 | -24.2 | -18.80 | 7.9 | -4.3 | -20.7 |
| Time Warner Inc. | A+ | -12.6 | -11.1 | -11.4 | -15.7 | 3.7 | -3.3 | -5.4 | -11.51 | 49.4 | -54.9 | |

| Company | Rating | | | | | | | | | | | |
|---|---|---|---|---|---|---|---|---|---|---|---|---|
| TRW Inc. | A+ | -9.6 | -11.7 | 0.6 | 3.9 | 7.0 | 2.0 | -8.6 | 2.81 | 57.9 | -6.5 | -6.3 |
| Union Carbide Corp. | A+ | -12.9 | -13.3 | -3.6 | 4.5 | 20.0 | 7.5 | 9.5 | -4.10 | -1.3 |  | 36.2 |
| UST Inc. | A+ | 6.7 | 39.0 | 38.0 | 60.1 | 71.4 | 75.0 | 67.8 | 69.46 | 71.6 | 82.7 |  |
| Westvaco Corp. | A+ | -6.4 | -6.4 | -8.7 | -3.7 | -0.1 | -2.1 | -8.0 | -7.86 | -8.7 | -2.9 |  |
| Whirlpool Corp. | A+ | -3.3 | -0.1 | -0.5 | 2.7 | -0.3 | -5.7 | -3.3 |  |  | 3.8 |  |
| WMX Technologies | A+ | -4.7 | 1.1 | -2.7 | 0.2 | 0.1 | -5.2 | -25.3 |  |  |  |  |
| Alcoa | A | -11.5 | -14.7 | -8.8 | -5.6 | 2.3 | -0.1 | -2.6 | -1.49 | 0.9 | 3.8 | 36.2 |
| Amerada Hess Corp. | A | -9.1 | -12.8 | -15.3 | -9.5 | -11.7 | -6.5 | -11.7 | 1.64 | -3.2 | 8.0 | -3.5 |
| Amgen Inc. | A | 20.4 | 14.3 | 5.1 | 11.9 | 19.1 | 19.1 | 16.6 | -14.02 | -0.4 | 13.0 | 6.5 |
| Baxter Intl Inc. | A | -2.4 | -6.2 | -7.0 | -0.9 | -5.1 | -0.3 | -5.7 | 16.05 | 20.9 | 18.5 | -8.5 |
| Chrysler Corp. | A | -12.9 | -8.4 | 1.5 | 13.3 | 1.0 | 6.9 | -2.2 | -0.30 | 1.4 | 4.2 | 19.8 |
| Circuit City Stores | A | -3.5 | 4.0 | 7.9 | 18.5 | 17.0 | 0.2 | -4.6 | -15.49 | -7.0 | -23.4 | 17.2 |
| Coca-Cola Co. | A | 14.6 | 16.3 | 23.3 | 33.2 | 29.5 | 35.5 | 27.2 | 24.94 | 17.8 | 24.9 | 20.0 |
| Corning Inc. | A | 1.2 | 1.5 | 5.1 | 14.4 | 8.2 | 11.4 | 15.2 | -2.29 | 1.0 | -7.5 | -22.0 |
| CSX Corp. | A | -10.6 | -11.6 | -4.5 | -1.7 | -1.5 | -1.8 | -0.9 | -2.78 | -3.9 | -2.0 | 41.2 |
| Dow Chemical | A | -3.2 | -3.4 | 2.3 | 7.6 | 9.0 | 5.5 | -1.9 | 2.17 | 1.7 | 2.4 | -56.7 |
| Eastman Kodak Co. | A | -3.3 | -0.4 | 1.4 | -1.1 | 12.1 | 32.3 | -6.4 | -4.93 | -2.3 | 45.6 | 1.7 |
| Enron Corp. | A | -5.1 | 0.6 | 0.5 | -3.7 | -2.6 | -2.6 | -3.1 | 0.11 | -3.9 | -5.5 | -4.7 |
| Honeywell Inc. | A | -9.3 | -1.1 | 7.5 | 13.9 | 17.4 | 10.7 | 6.3 | 12.66 | 25.6 | 13.9 | 2.5 |
| Lilly (Eli) & Co. | A | 9.3 | -4.9 | 2.9 | 8.7 | 14.3 | 7.9 | -9.4 | 16.87 | 24.8 | 25.2 | 2.0 |
| Occidental Petrol | A | -11.6 | 11.3 | -3.2 | -8.0 | -3.5 | -4.7 | -18.9 | -10.67 | -1.5 | 13.4 | 23.7 |
| Parker-Hannifin | A | -9.3 | -4.9 | -2.9 | -7.4 | 4.5 | -0.2 | -3.1 | -0.36 | -0.2 | 5.7 | 6.4 |
| Phelps Dodge Corp. | A | -1.0 | 9.6 | -1.1 | -0.5 | 16.0 | 1.4 | -0.4 | -8.50 | -16.0 | -8.7 | 3.1 |
| Procter & Gamble | A | 1.6 | 0.3 | -9.2 | 7.0 | 10.6 | 9.5 | 5.1 | 9.35 | 13.5 | 22.3 | -13.9 |
| Ryder System Inc. | A | -2.2 | -3.5 | -1.1 | 2.0 | 2.7 | -2.3 | -1.6 | -1.1 | 0.2 | -5.4 | 23.3 |
| Sara Lee Corp. | A | -1.3 | 0.6 | 0.9 | -3.4 | -0.6 | 0.6 | -2.1 | -10.9 | 10.1 | 15.0 | -3.8 |
| Tenneco Inc. | A | -15.7 | -4.3 | -0.3 | 3.9 | -9.3 | -13.6 | 2.1 | -1.7 | -20.2 | -0.9 | 20.0 |
| Texaco Inc. | A | -3.9 | -4.5 | -1.9 | -5.0 | -10.3 | 5.4 | 13.5 | -8.3 | -1.0 | 6.3 | -5.1 |
| Textron Inc. | A | -0.4 | -0.4 | 0.1 | -2.6 | 8.5 | 9.1 | 0.3 | -3.4 | -4.1 | -1.5 | -1.3 |

Table B.1  Continued

| Company name | CalPERS grade | 1991 | 1992 | 1993 | 1994 | 1995 | 1996 | 1997 | 1998 | 1999 | 2000 | 2001 |
|---|---|---|---|---|---|---|---|---|---|---|---|---|
| Unocal Corp. | A | -11.4 | -7.9 | -7.0 | -12.5 | -5.1 | -6.4 | -1.6 | -11.6 | -5.7 | 10.5 | 3.4 |
| Air Products & Chemicals | B | -1.0 | -3.5 | -6.4 | -6.9 | -2.3 | -3.6 | -3.9 | -6.6 | -6.5 | -2.4 | -0.6 |
| Anheuser-Busch Cos Inc. | B | -0.1 | -5.6 | -3.8 | 7.0 | 2.2 | 7.0 | 5.1 | 2.9 | 7.7 | 13.8 | 19.2 |
| ADP | B | 4.8 | 6.5 | 27.1 | 32.4 | 33.3 | 43.8 | 10.5 | 10.2 | 5.6 | 12.5 | 14.2 |
| Boeing Co. | B | -1.0 | 0.7 | 1.9 | 2.8 | -3.5 | 0.2 | -10.3 | -9.2 | 0.3 | 6.3 | 17.7 |
| Burlington Northern Santa Fe | B | -11.0 | -7.9 | -0.8 | 53.1 | 53.2 | 0.1 | -3.7 | -2.5 | -3.0 | -2.1 | 0.1 |
| Computer Associates Intl Inc. | B | -1.5 | 12.3 | 28.5 | 53.1 | 76.3 | 51.2 | 71.2 | 52.1 | 106.7 | -40.4 | -54.4 |
| Emerson Electric Co. | B | 5.6 | 11.0 | 11.0 | 8.4 | 15.2 | 15.1 | 10.5 | 13.2 | 15.6 | 19.4 | 15.3 |
| Fluor Corp. | B | -12.6 | -21.0 | -10.2 | 3.4 | 4.3 | 3.2 | -12.4 | -3.8 | -3.9 | -14.7 | 1.6 |
| Georgia-Pacific Corp. | B | -12.2 | -0.1 | -5.3 | 0.4 | 10.8 | -2.8 | -12.3 | -9.5 | 0.5 | 5.0 | -5.2 |
| Goodyear Tire & Rubber | B | -5.5 | -8.5 | 9.3 | 5.0 | 3.2 | 0.5 | 0.6 | -1.2 | -7.9 | -6.3 | -7.1 |
| Great Lakes Chemical | B | 12.6 | 14.5 | 21.7 | 14.8 | 11.7 | 5.1 | -6.5 | -4.5 | -2.7 | -3.1 | -18.4 |
| Motorola Inc. | B | -11.3 | -3.1 | 5.8 | 4.6 | 8.3 | -4.6 | -6.3 | -20.7 | 4.0 | -22.3 | -25.3 |
| Nordstrom Inc. | B | -9.3 | -11.1 | -13.0 | -7.7 | -4.7 | -6.5 | -8.8 | -6.1 | -3.5 | -7.0 | -7.0 |
| Service Corp Intl. | B | 24.2 | 16.8 | 29.7 | 10.6 | 14.0 | 11.2 | 11.8 | 5.1 | -3.1 | -19.5 | -8.5 |
| Times Mirror Company | B | -10.5 | -12.4 | 3.6 | -15.1 | -13.1 | -6.6 | 8.0 | 30.4 | 10.9 |  |  |
| Xerox Corp. | B | 10.7 | -10.8 | 24.8 | 9.2 | 13.4 | 12.8 | 9.1 | 10.3 | 6.3 | -7.7 | -4.7 |
| Abbott Laboratories | C | 10.1 | 10.7 | 10.8 | 20.1 | 22.1 | 19.4 | 16.8 | 21.4 | 18.4 | 23.7 | 28.3 |
| Compaq Computer Corp. | C | -9.3 | -5.6 | 5.4 | 8.1 | 7.1 | 8.8 | 2.4 | -28.5 | -14.8 | 1.8 | -15.9 |
| Donnelley (R R) & Sons Co. | C | -5.7 | -0.7 | -7.8 | -2.7 | 0.4 | -10.0 | -2.1 | 0.1 | -0.4 | 1.6 | 0.8 |
| General Electric Co. | C | -3.4 | -3.6 | -2.4 | -0.6 | 1.9 | -2.0 | -3.7 | -2.9 | -5.4 | -5.4 | 0.4 |
| Genuine Parts Co. | C | 3.3 | 6.0 | 9.9 | 7.4 | 8.5 | 8.2 | 9.1 | 5.3 | 4.6 | 3.9 | 7.1 |
| Gillette Co. | C | 6.5 | 1.9 | 8.3 | 23.5 | 15.3 | 40.0 | 16.2 | 7.0 | 0.9 | 4.7 | 13.3 |
| Hercules Inc. | C | -7.1 | -10.4 | -3.1 | 5.3 | 3.4 | 10.8 | -0.7 | 5.5 | 6.1 | -3.5 | 5.6 |
| Home Depot Inc. | C | -0.9 | 3.9 | 3.7 | 3.9 | 3.7 | 6.3 | 3.2 | 4.0 | 4.6 | 2.4 | 2.5 |

| | | | | | | | | | | | | |
|---|---|---|---|---|---|---|---|---|---|---|---|---|
| Homestake Mining | C | -22.4 | -6.2 | -1.6 | 0.8 | 4.0 | -5.2 | -26.9 | -21.9 | -14.6 | -18.0 | |
| Mallinckrodt Group Inc. | C | -5.5 | -8.8 | -8.3 | -1.1 | -2.3 | -5.4 | 9.0 | -3.7 | 0.1 | 8.3 | 21.2 |
| Mattel Inc. | C | 5.9 | 21.1 | 23.2 | 19.7 | 21.8 | 15.0 | 16.2 | 4.8 | -3.7 | | |
| Morton International | C | | -0.8 | -5.2 | 5.7 | 7.3 | 7.3 | -0.3 | 0.1 | | | |
| Norfolk Southern Corp. | C | -13.1 | -2.7 | -9.1 | -3.0 | -3.0 | -2.0 | -6.7 | -2.8 | -5.4 | -2.4 | 0.3 |
| Pepsico Inc. | C | 5.4 | 8.3 | 8.2 | 5.9 | 5.9 | 2.5 | 2.0 | 13.6 | -9.1 | 46.2 | 78.3 |
| Royal Dutch Pet. (NY Reg.) | C | -8.5 | -11.3 | -7.5 | -7.8 | -4.7 | -3.3 | -8.6 | -3.5 | 9.4 | 12.8 | 15.8 |
| Tandy Corp. | C | -6.8 | -9.4 | -6.1 | -6.7 | 0.5 | -8.6 | 4.3 | -1.9 | 14.5 | 14.6 | 1.3 |
| Union Pacific Corp. | C | -7.0 | -3.3 | -3.5 | -4.6 | 0.7 | 13.4 | -5.4 | -9.2 | -3.7 | -0.9 | 1.4 |
| Weyerhaeuser Co. | C | -7.3 | 3.5 | 7.4 | 0.4 | 4.4 | -1.5 | -8.5 | -10.5 | -3.6 | -4.9 | -6.5 |
| Albertsons Inc. | D | 5.3 | 10.4 | 6.3 | 9.6 | 11.1 | 15.2 | 9.7 | 8.6 | 11.9 | 4.3 | 5.8 |
| Ford Motor Co. | D | -4.9 | -3.9 | -0.2 | 1.1 | 1.5 | 0.8 | 1.5 | 1.3 | -1.6 | -1.8 | -5.3 |
| Intel Corp. | D | -5.9 | 4.2 | 17.9 | 15.7 | 21.1 | 21.6 | 12.4 | 3.0 | 19.8 | -0.1 | -18.4 |
| Kellogg Co. | D | 7.5 | 3.2 | 13.1 | 22.0 | 13.2 | 15.0 | 11.5 | 10.1 | 9.5 | 16.6 | 43.5 |
| Minnesota Mining & Mfg. | D | -1.5 | 5.2 | 7.1 | 4.5 | 2.8 | 2.9 | 6.2 | 7.1 | 12.1 | 13.4 | 11.2 |
| Pitney Bowes Inc. | D | 7.1 | -0.2 | 13.3 | 13.6 | 24.3 | 21.5 | 20.6 | 10.9 | 17.6 | 14.5 | 21.5 |
| Placer Dome Inc. | D | -20.3 | -6.8 | -13.5 | -15.7 | -19.0 | -20.1 | -34.6 | -13.5 | -13.5 | -15.7 | -8.7 |
| Rubbermaid Inc. | D | -2.2 | -6.4 | -1.6 | -1.7 | -6.8 | -0.2 | -1.5 | -1.8 | | | |
| Schering-Plough | D | 9.1 | 9.4 | 14.5 | 21.7 | 26.0 | 21.0 | 19.3 | 26.8 | 25.8 | 28.4 | 24.3 |
| American Home Products | F | 23.5 | 21.9 | 24.5 | 20.1 | 18.4 | 24.1 | 27.7 | 28.4 | 15.6 | 28.0 | |
| Atlantic Richfield Co. | F | -5.9 | -2.4 | -4.5 | -2.9 | -3.2 | 0.9 | -0.5 | -15.7 | -0.6 | | |
| Du Pont (E I) De Nemours | F | -10.3 | -13.4 | -5.9 | -2.1 | 1.2 | 4.1 | -0.3 | -7.1 | -1.5 | 1.7 | 4.19 |
| Gannett Co. | F | -0.7 | -8.2 | 20.1 | 16.4 | 38.5 | 23.0 | 29.7 | 30.3 | 35.8 | 24.3 | 37.1 |
| Johnson & Johnson | F | 8.1 | 5.4 | 9.0 | 14.4 | 16.1 | 19.1 | 14.4 | 17.8 | 20.0 | 25.2 | 32.9 |
| United Technologies | F | -19.6 | -9.1 | 0.2 | 2.3 | 2.7 | 4.8 | 5.3 | 8.4 | 5.2 | 10.1 | 20.1 |

Table B.2 Average EVA™ by CalPERS grade groups, weighted by companies' assets (per cent)

| CalPERS grade | Economic value added (EVA™) | | | |
|---|---|---|---|---|
| | 1991–93 | 1994–96 | 1997–99 | 2000–1 |
| A+ | –2.73 | 4.94 | 5.63 | 9.14 |
| A, B | –1.42 | 5.92 | 2.59 | 2.80 |
| C, D, F | –2.60 | 2.73 | –0.40 | 2.73 |

Table B.3 Average differential spread by CalPERS grade groups (per cent)

| CalPERS grade | Differential spread | | | | | | | | | | | Arithmetic mean, 1991–2001 |
|---|---|---|---|---|---|---|---|---|---|---|---|---|
| | 1991 | 1992 | 1993 | 1994 | 1995 | 1996 | 1997 | 1998 | 1999 | 2000 | 2001 | |
| A+ | 0.07 | –0.08 | –0.07 | 1.28 | 0.93 | 0.64 | 1.63 | 2.31 | 3.83 | 3.03 | 2.60 | 1.47 |
| A, B | 0.43 | 0.24 | 2.14 | 1.38 | 1.70 | 0.65 | –1.43 | –0.70 | 0.23 | –2.99 | –5.78 | –0.38 |
| C, D, F | 0.68 | 0.25 | 0.43 | –0.21 | –0.11 | –0.32 | 0.64 | 0.49 | –3.04 | 0.17 | –0.07 | –0.04 |

*Table B.4*   Average differential spread by CalPERS grade groups, for a three-year period (per cent)

| CalPERS grade | Differential spread | | | |
|---|---|---|---|---|
| | 1991–93 | 1994–96 | 1997–99 | 2000–1 |
| A+ | −0.03 | 0.94 | 2.63 | 2.81 |
| A, B | 0.99 | 1.23 | −0.65 | −4.28 |
| C, D, F | 0.45 | 0.02 | −0.75 | 0.05 |

# References

ABA Committee on Corporate Laws, Section of Business Law. *Corporate Directors' Guidebook* (2nd edn, 1994).

Agrawal, Anup and Charles R. Knoeber. 'Firm Performance and Mechanisms to Control Agency Problems between Managers and Shareholders', *Journal of Financial and Quantitative Analysis*, 31(3) (September 1996).

Allen, William T. (Chancellor, Delaware Court of Chancery). 'Redefining the Role of Outside Directors in an Age of Global Competition', Speech at Ray Garrett, Jr, Corporate and Securities Law Institute, Northwestern University, 30 April 1992. Quoted in Robert A.G. Monks and Nell Minow, *Corporate Governance* (Blackwell Publishers, 1995).

—— Letter to Ira M. Millstein, 7 January 1993. On file with the authors.

—— Memorandum to the 1993 Tulane Corporate Law Institute 11, undated. On file with the authors.

American Federation of Labor and Congress of Industrial Organizations (AFL-CIO). *Investing in Our Future: AFL-CIO Proxy Voting Guidelines* (1997).

American Law Institute. *Principles of Corporate Governance* (1994). First published 1983.

*Aronson* v. *Lewis*, 473 A.2d 805, 816 (Del. 1984).

'Ashland Political Payments Made Abroad, Facts on File', *World News Digest*, 19 July 1975.

Bacidore, Jeffrey, John Boquist, Todd Milbourn and Anjan Thakor. 'The Search for the Best Financial Performance Measure', *Financial Analysts Journal*, 53 (May/June 1997).

Bagley, Constance E. and Richard H. Koppes. 'Leader of the Pack: A Proposal for Disclosure of Board Leadership Structure', *San Diego Law Review*, 34 (1997).

Baliga, B. Ram, R. Charles Moyer and Ramesh S. Rao. 'CEO Duality and Firm Performance: What's All the Fuss?', *Strategic Management Journal*, 17 (1996).

Barclay, Michael J. and Clifford G. Holderness. 'Control of Corporations by Active Block Investors', *Journal of Applied Corporate Finance* (Fall 1991).

Barnhart, Scott W. and Stuart Rosenstein. 'Board Composition, Managerial Ownership, and Firm Performance: An Empirical Analysis', *Financial Review*, 33 (1998).

'Barons of Bankruptcy', *Financial Times*, 31 July 2002.

Baysinger, Barry D. and Henry N. Butler. 'Revolution versus Evolution in Corporation Law: The ALI's Project and the Independent Director', *George Washington Law Review*, 52 (1984).

—— 'Corporate Governance and the Boards of Directors: Performance Effects of Changes in Board Composition', *Journal of Law, Economics and Organization*, 1 (1985).

Belair, Felix Jr. 'SEC Petition re Mattel' (Abstract of article), *The New York Times*, 3 October 1974.

*Benerofe* v. *Cha*, 1996 WL 535405, at *7 (Del. Ch. 12 Sept. 1996), subsequent proceedings, 1998 WL 83081 (Del. Ch. 20 Feb. 1998).

Berle, Adolph and Gardiner Means. *The Modern Corporation and Private Property* (Macmillan, 1932).

Bhagat, Sanjai and Bernard Black. 'The Uncertain Relationship Between Board Composition and Firm Performance', *Business Lawyer*, 54 (1999).

—— 'Board Independence and Long Term Firm Performance', Working Paper (February 2000). Available via http://papers.ssrn.com.

Bhagat, Sanjai, Dennis C. Carey and Charles M. Elson. 'Director Ownership, Corporate Performance, and Management Turnover', *Business Lawyer*, 54 (1999).

Black, Bernard S. 'Shareholder Activism and Corporate Governance in the United States', in Peter Newman (ed.), *The New Palgrave Dictionary of Economics and the Law* (Palgrave, 1998).

Block, Dennis J., Nancy E. Barton and Stephen A. Radin. *The Business Judgment Rule: Fiduciary Duties of Corporate Directors* (5th edn, 1998), *Supplement* (Aspen Law and Business, 2002).

Bowsher, Charles A. (Chairman, Public Oversight Board). *Accounting and Investor Protection Issues Raised by Enron and Other Public Companies: Hearing Before the Senate Comm. on Banking, Housing, and Urban Affairs*, 107th Cong. 2 (2002).

Boyd, Brian K. 'Board Control and CEO Compensation', *Strategic Management Journal*, 15 (1994).

*Brehm* v. *Eisner*, 746 A.2d 244, 264, n.66 (Del. 2000).

Brickley, James A., Jeffery L. Coles and Gregg Jarrell. 'Leadership Structure: Separating the CEO and Chairman of the Board', *Journal of Corporate Finance*, 3 (1997).

Brickley, James A., Jeffery L. Coles and Rory L. Terry. 'Outside Directors and the Adoption of Poison Pills', *Journal of Financial Economics*, 35 (1994).

Brudney, Victor. 'The Independent Director – Heavenly City or Potemkin Village?', *Harvard Law Review*, 95 (1982).

Business Roundtable, The. *Statement of the Business Round Table on Corporate Governance* (September 1997).

—— *Statement of the Business Round Table on Corporate Governance Principles Relating to the Enron Bankruptcy* (February 2002).

Byrd, John W. and Kent A. Hickman, 'Do Outside Directors Monitor Managers? Evidence from Tender Offer Bids', *Journal of Financial Economics* (1992).

Cadbury Committee. *Report of the Committee on the Financial Aspects of Corporate Governance* (Cadbury Report). December 1992. Reissued April 1996. Combined with other reports into publication by the London Stock Exchange (LSE), *Principles of Good Governance and Code of Best Practice (The Combined Code)* (London Stock Exchange, 1998).

CalPERS. 'CalPERS Announces Results of Governance Survey.' Press Release, 31 May 1995. On file with the authors.

—— *Company Responses to Request for Board Governance Self-Evaluation – Final Report* (May 1995).

—— 'Responses, Final Report: Company Responses to Request for Board Governance Self-Evaluation' (1995). On file with the authors.

—— *Corporate Governance Core Principles and Guidelines: The United States* (April 1998).

*Caremark International Inc. Derivative Litig.*, 698 A.2d 959, 967 (Del. Ch. 1996).

Carleton, Willard T., James M. Nelson and Michael S. Weisbach. 'The Influence of Institutions on Corporate Governance through Private Negotiations: Evidence from TIAA-CREF', *Journal of Finance*, 53 (1998).

Chaganti, Rajeswararao S., Subash Sharma and Vijay Mahajan. 'Corporate Board Size, Composition and Corporate Failures in Retailing Industry', *Journal of Management Studies*, 22 (1985).

Chandler, Alfred D. Jr. *The Visible Hand: The Managerial Revolution in American Business* (Harvard University Press, 1977).

Chandler, William B., III and Leo E. Strine, Jr. 'The New Federalism of The American Corporate Governance System: Preliminary Reflections of Two Residents of One Small State', Prepared for Penn Law and Economics Institute Conference on Control Transactions, 8–9 February 2003 [draft]. Available on line at http://papers.ssrn.com/abstract = 367720.

Clurman, Richard M. *Who's in Charge?* (Whittle Direct Communications, 1994).

Conference Board, The. *The Corporate Board: A Growing Role in Strategic Assessment* (Conference Board, 1996).

—— *Commission on Public Trust and Enterprise: Findings and Recommendations* (Conference Board, 2003).

Copeland, Thomas E. and J. Fred Weston. *Financial Theory and Corporate Policy* (3rd edn, Addison-Wesley, 1988).

Copeland, Thomas E., Tim Koller and Jack Murin. *Valuation: Measuring and Managing the Value of Companies*. (3rd edn, John Wiley & Sons, 1995).

Core, J., R. Holthausen and D. Larker. 'Corporate Governance, CEO Compensation, and Firm Performance', *Journal of Financial Economics*, 51 (1999).

Cotter, James F., Anil Shivdasani and Marc Zenner. 'Do Independent Directors Enhance Target Shareholder Wealth During Tender Offers?', *Journal of Financial Economics*, 43 (1997).

Council of Institutional Investors (CII). *Core Policies, General Principles, Positions and Explanatory Notes* (March 1998). Subsequently revised March 2002.

Council on Competitiveness. *Capital Choices: Changing the Way America Invests in Industry* (1992).

Cyert, Richard, Sok-Hyon Kang, Praveen Kumar and Anish Shah. 'Corporate Governance, Ownership Structure and CEO Compensation', Working Paper (1997).

Darwin, Charles. *On the Origin of Species by Means of Natural Selection* (1859).

'Deals Within Telecom Deals', 'Bubble Beneficiaries', *New York Times*, 25 August 2002.

Del Guercio, Diane and Jennifer Hawkins. 'The Motivation and Impact of Pension Fund Activism', *Journal of Financial Economics*, 52 (1999).

Del. Code Ann. tit. 8, § 141(a) and II.B (1974).

Denis, David J. and Diane K. Denis. 'Performance Changes Following Top Management Dismissals', *Journal of Financial Economics*, 50 (1995).

Denis, David J., Diane K. Denis and Atulya Sarin. 'Agency Problems, Equity Ownership and Corporate Diversification', *Journal of Finance*, 52 (1997).

Dennett, Daniel C. *Darwin's Dangerous Idea* (Simon & Shuster; London: Allen Lane, 1995).

Dobrzynski, Judith H. 'At GM, A Magna Carta for Directors', *Business Week*, 4 April 1994.

Donaldson, Gordon. 'A New Tool for Boards: The Strategic Audit', *Harvard Business Review* (July–August 1995).

Douglas, William, O. 'Directors who do not Direct', *Harvard Law Review*, 47 (1305), 1934.

Eggleston, W.N. 'Executive Summary, Letter to Senators Linus and Collins re: PSI Report No. 107-70 [Report of the Permanent Subcommittee on Investigations, *The Role of the Board of Directors in Enron's Collapse*, July 8, 2002]', 1 August 2002. 8 Del. C. § 102(b)(7).

'End of the Directors' Rubber Stamp', *Business Week*, 10 September 1979.

'Enron Papers Show Big Profits on Price Belts', *New York Times*, 12 December 2002. On line at NYTimes.com.

'Enron's Real Financials', *Forbes*, 3 February 2003. On line at Forbes.com.

Fama, Eugene F. 'Agency Problems and the Theory of the Firm', *Journal of Political Economics*, 88 (1980).

Fama, Eugene F. and Michael Jensen. 'Separation of Ownership and Control', *Journal of Law and Economics*, 26 (1983).

Farrell, Kathleen A. and David A. Whidbee. 'The Consequences of Forced CEO Succession for Outside Directors', *Journal of Business*, 73(4) (2000).

Forjan, James M. 'The Wealth Effects of Shareholder-Sponsored Proposals', *Revised Financial Economics*, 8 (1999).

Geddes, R. Richard and Hrishikesh D. Vinod. 'CEO Age and Outside Directors: A Hazard Analysis', *Review of Industrial Organization*, 6(1) (1996).

General Motors Board of Directors. *GM Board of Directors Corporate Governance Guidelines on Significant Corporate Governance Issues* (January 1994), subsequently revised.

Gertner, Robert and Steven N. Kaplan. *The Value Maximizing Board*, University of Chicago and National Bureau of Economic Research. Working Paper (1996).

Gibbons, Robert and Kevin J. Murphy. 'Optimal Incentive Contracts in the Presence of Career Concerns: Theory and Evidence', *Journal of Political Economics*, 100 (1992).

Gillan, Stuart L. and Laura T. Starks. 'A Survey of Shareholder Activism: Motivation and Empirical Evidence', *Contemporary Finance Digest*, 2 (Autumn 1998).

—— 'Corporate Governance Proposals and Shareholder Activism: The Role of Institutional Investors', *Journal of Financial Economics*, 57 (2000).

Gillies, James. *Boardroom Renaissance: Power, Morality and Performance in the Modern Corporation* (Ontario, McGraw-Hill, 1992).

Goodman, Amy L. 'Institutional Investors Come of Age', *Insights*, 4(2) (December 1990).

Gopinath, C., Julie I. Siciliano and Robert L. Murray. 'Changing Role of the Board of Directors: In Search of a New Strategic Identity?', *Mid-Atlantic Journal of Business*, 30 (1994).

*Gotham Partners, L.P. v. Hallwood Realty Partners, L.P.*, 2002 WL 31303135 (Del. 29 Aug. 2002).

*Grobow v. Perot*, 539 A.2d 180, 188–92 (Del. 1988).

*Guth v. Loft*, 5 A.2d 503 (Del. 1939).

Hall, Brian J. and Jeffrey B. Liebman. 'Are CEO's Really Paid Like Bureaucrats?', *Quarterly Journal of Economics*, 113 (1998).

*Hanson Trust PLC v. SCM Acquisition, Inc.*, 781 F.2d 264, 275 (2nd Cir. 1986).

Harford, Jarrad. 'Takeover Bids and Target Directors' Incentives: Retention, Experience and Settling-Up', Working Paper, University of Oregon (2000).

Helms, Bradley A. with Richard Koppes. 'Statistical Alchemy: how methodological shortcomings in the inquiries into the financial impact of corporate governance reform prevent the Wall Streets of the world from reaching a consensus about the value of good corporate governance', *Business Law International* (2000), 218.

Hermalin, Benjamin E. and Michael S. Weisbach. 'The Effects of Board Composition and Direct Incentives on Firm Performance', *Financial Management*, 20 (1991).

—— 'Boards of Directors as Endogenously Chosen Institutions: A Survey of the Economic Literature', Unpublished manuscript available on line at http://www.nber.org/papers/w8161 (posted March 2001).

Higgs, Derek. *Review of the Role and Effectiveness of Non-Executive Directors* (Higgs Report), 20 January 2003.

Holmström, Bengt. 'Managerial Incentive Schemes – A Dynamic Perspective', in *Essays in Economics and Management in Honor of Lars Wahlbeck* (Swenska Handelshögkolan, 1982).

Ibbotson Associates. Table C-1 of *Stocks, Bonds, Bills and Inflation 2002 Yearbook* (2002).

*In re Abbott Labs. Derivative S'holders Litig.*, 293 F.3d 378 (7th Cir.), withdrawn, 299 F.3d 898 (7th Cir. 2002) [New Abbott opinion forthcoming].

*In re Caremark Int'l Inc. Derivative Litig.*, 698 A.2d 959, 967 (Del. Ch. 1996).

*In re The Walt Disney Co. Derivative Litig.*, Del. Ch., C.A. No. 15452, Chandler, C., Memorandum Opinion (May 28, 2003).

Ingrassia, Paul J. and Joseph B. White. *Comeback: The Fall and Rise of the American Automobile Industry* (Simon & Schuster, 1994).

*Ivanhoe Partners* v. *Newmont Mining Corp.*, 535 A.2d 1,334, 1,341, 1,343 (Del. 1987).

Jackson, Alfred. 'The How and Why of EVA™ at CS First Boston', *Journal of Applied Corporate Finance* (Spring 1996).

Jensen, Michael C. and William H. Meckling. 'Theory of the Firm: Managerial Behavior, Agency Costs and Ownership Structure', *Journal of Financial Economics*, 3 (1976).

Jensen, Michael C. and Kevin J. Murphy. 'CEO Incentives: It's Not How Much You Pay, But How', *Harvard Business Review*, 3 (May–June 1990).

—— 'Performance Pay and Top-Management Incentives', *Journal of Political Economics*, 98 (1990).

Karpoff, Jonathan, Paul Malatesta and Ralph Walkling, 'Corporate Governance and Shareholder Initiatives: Empirical Evidence', *Journal of Financial Economics*, 42 (1996).

Korn/Ferry International. *Board Meeting in Session: 23rd Annual Board of Directors Study* (1996).

—— *28th Annual Board of Directors Study* (2001).

Kravets, David. 'Key Enron Trader Pleads Guilty', Associated Press, 17 October 2002. On line at http://finance.news.com.au/common/printpage/0,6093,5311657,00.html

Lanner, Curt (CS First Boston Corporation). 'Enron Corp., ENE "Strong Buy"', 26 January 2001.

Lee, Chun I., Stuart Rosenstein, Nanda Rangan and Wallace N. Davidson, III. 'Board Composition and Shareholder Wealth: The Case of Management Buy-outs', *Financial Management* (Spring 1992).

*Levco Alternative Fund Ltd.* v. *Reader's Digest Ass'n, Inc.*, 2002 WL 1859064 (Del. 13 Aug. 2002).

Lewellen, Wilber G. 'A Pure Financial Rationale for the Conglomerate Merger', *Journal of Finance* (May 1971).

*Lewis* v. *S.L. and E., Inc.*, 629 F.2d 764, 769 (2d Cir. 1980).

Lintner, John. 'Expectations, Mergers and Equilibrium in Purely Competitive Securities Markets', *American Economic Review* (May 1971).

Loomis, Carol J. 'Dinosaurs?', *Fortune*, 3 May 1993.

Lubin, Joann S. 'Splitting Posts Of Chairman, CEO Catches On', *Wall Street Journal*, 11 November 2002, at B1.

MacAvoy, Paul W. and Jean W. Rosenthal. *Cost Containment Strategies and Nuclear Plant Safety: The Experience at Northeast Utilities* (Forthcoming) (2003).

MacAvoy, Paul W., Scott Cantor, Jim Dana and Sarah Peck. 'ALI Proposals for Increased Control of the Corporation by the Board of Directors: An Economic Analysis', in *Statement of the Business Roundtable on the American Law Institute's Proposed 'Principles of Corporate Governance and Structure: Restatement and Recommendations'* (1983).

Mallette, Paul and Karen Fowler. 'Effects of Board Composition and Stock Ownership on the Adoption of "Poison Pills"', *Academic Management Journal*, 35 (1992).

Mayer, Allan J. 'Washington Money-Go-Round', *Newsweek*, 8 December 1975.

*McCall* v. *Scott*, 239 F.3d 808 (6th Cir.), modified, 250 F.3d 997 (6th Cir. 2001).

Mehran, Hamid. 'Executive Compensation Structure, Ownership and Firm Performance', *Journal of Financial Economics*, 38 (1995).

Mehran, Hamid, George E. Nogler and Kenneth B. Schwartz. 'CEO Incentive Plans and Corporate Liquidation Policy', *Journal of Financial Economics*, 50 (1998).

Melicher, Ronald W. and David F. Rush. 'Evidence on the Acquisition-Related Performance of Conglomerate Firms'. *The Journal of Finance*, 29(1) (March 1974).

Mikkelson, Wayne H. and M. Megan Partch. 'The Decline of Takeovers and Disciplinary Managerial Turnover', *Journal of Financial Economics*, 22 (1997).

Micklethwait, John and Adrian Wooldridge. *The Company: A Short History of a Revolutionary Idea*. (Random House, Inc., 2003)

Miller, Michael W. and Laurence Hooper. 'Signing Off', *Wall Street Journal*, 27 January 1993.

*Mills Acquisition Co.* v. *MacMillan, Inc.*, 559 A.2d 1,261, 1,279–80 (Del. 1989).

Millstein, Ira M. 'The Evolution of the Certifying Board', *Business Lawyer*, 48 (1993).

—— 'The State of Corporate Governance', Speech Before the National Association of Corporate Directors, 1 November 1993, in Robert A.G. Monks and Nell Minow. *Corporate Governance* (Blackwell, 1995).

—— 'The Professional Board', *Business Lawyer*, 50 (1995).

—— 'Director Professionalism', Report of the NACD Blue Ribbon Commission, (1996, updated and reprinted 2001).

—— 'The Responsible Board', *Business Lawyer*, 52 (1997).

Millstein, Ira M. and Paul W. MacAvoy. 'The Active Board of Directors and Performance of the Large Publicly Traded Corporation', *Columbia Law Review*, 98 (June 1998).

Mitsui Life Symposium. 'EVA™ and Shareholder Value in Japan: Fourth Mitsui Life Symposium on Global Financial Markets', *Journal of Applied Corporate Finance* (Winter 1997).

*MM Cos.* v. *Liquid Audio, Inc.*, No. 606, 2002 (Del. 7 Jan. 2003).

*Moran* v. *Household Int'l, Inc.*, 500 A.2d 1,346, 1,356 (Del. 1985).

Mueller, Dennis C. 'A Theory of Conglomerate Mergers', *The Quarterly Journal of Economics*, 83(4) (November 1969).

NACD. *Report of the Blue Ribbon Commission on Performance Evaluation of Chief Executive Officers, Boards and Directors* (1994).

—— *Report of the Blue Ribbon Commission on Director Professionalism* (November 1996). Reissued 2001.

—— *Report of the Blue Ribbon Commission on the Role of the Board in Corporate Strategy* (September 2000).

—— *Public Company Governance Survey* (November 2001).

NASDAQ. 'Affected Marketplace Rules: 4200(a)(14), 4200(a)(15), 4350(c), 4350(d), and IM-4350-4', 9 October 2002, Available on line at http://www.nasdaq.com/about/2002_141.pdf.

New York Stock Exchange. 'Corporate Governance Rule Proposals Reflecting Recommendations from the NYSE Corporate Accountability and Listing Standards Committee', 16 August 2002. Available on line at http://www.nyse.com/pdfs/corp_gov_pro_b.pdf.

—— *Listed Company Manual § 303.01(B)(2)(a)* (December 1999).

*New York Times* Business/Financial Desk, 13 February 2002.

O'Byrne, Stephen F. 'EVA™ and Market Value', *Journal of Applied Corporate Finance* (Spring 1996).

*OmniCare, Inc. v. NCS Healthcare, Inc.*, 2002 WL 31767892 (Del. 10 Dec. 2002).

Oster, Sharon. *Modern Competitive Analysis* (2nd edn, Oxford University Press, 1994).

Pantaleo, Peter V. and Barry W. Ridings. 'Reorganization Value', *Business Lawyer*, 51 (1996).

*Paramount Communications, Inc. v. Time Inc.*, 571 A.2d 1,140, 1,150–51 Del. Ch. (Del. 1990), aff'g 1989 WL 79880, at *19 (14 July 1989).

Partnoy, Frank (Professor of Law, University of San Diego School of Law). Testimony in response to the US Senate Committee on Governmental Affairs, 24 January 2002. On line at http://www.senate.gov/~gov_affairs/012402partnoy.htm.

Pearl Meyer Partners. *2001 Proxy Research* (New York: Private distribution).

Perry, Tod. 'Incentive Compensation for Outside Directors and CEO Turnover', Working Paper. (July 2000). Available on line at http://papers.ssrn.com.

Pi, L. and S.G. Timme. 'Corporate Control and Bank Efficiency', *Banking and Finance*, 17 (1993).

Plender, John, *Going off the Rails: Global Capital as the Crisis of Legitimacy* (Wiley, 2003).

Pound, John. 'Corporate Governance Affects Corporate Strategy', *Corporate Board* (July–August 1994).

Pulliam, Susan and Steven Lipin. 'Some Major American Express Holders Voice Disappointment About Robinson', *Wall Street Journal*, 29 January 1993.

Ragazzo, Robert A. 'Unifying the Law of Hostile Takeovers: The Impact of QVC and its Progeny', *Houston Law Review*, 32 (1995).

*Rales v. Blasband*, 634 A.2d 927, 936 (Del. 1993).

Rappaport, Alfred. *Creating Shareholder Value: The New Standard for Business Performance* (The Free Press, 1986).

Rechner, Paula L. and Dan R. Dalton. 'CEO Duality and Organizational Performance: A Longitudinal Analysis', *Strategic Management Journal*, 12 (1991).

Rediker, Kenneth J. and Anju Seth. 'Boards of Directors and Substitution Effects of Alternative Governance Mechanisms', *Strategic Management Journal*, 16 (1995).

*Revlon, Inc.* v. *MacAndrews and Forbes Holdings, Inc.*, 506 A.2d 173, 182 (Del. 1986).

Romano, Roberta. 'Less is More: Making Institutional Investor Activism a Valuable Mechanism of Corporate Governance', Working Paper. Available on line at http//:papers.ssrn.com (2000).

Rosen, Sherwin. 'Prizes and Incentives in Elimination Tournaments', *American Economic Review*, 76, 701–15 (1986).

Ross, Irwin. 'The 1996 Stern Stewart Performance 1000', *Journal of Applied Corporate Finance* (Winter 1997).

Russell Reynolds Associates and The Wirthlin Group. *Redefining Corporate Governance: 1995 U.S. Survey of Institutional Investors* (1995). See also Wirthlin Worldwide and Russell Reynolds Associates.

*Saito* v. *McKesson HBOC, Inc.*, 806 A.2d 113 (Del. 11 June 2002).

Sarbanes–Oxley Act of 2002 (H.R. 3763). Signed by the President 30 July 2002.

Scherer, F.M. and David Ross. *Industrial Market Structure and Economic Performance* (3rd edn, 1990).

Scott, Kenneth E. and Allan W. Kleidon. 'CEO Performance, Board Types, and Board Performance: A First Cut', in T. Baums, R.M. Buxbaum and K.J. Hopt (eds), *Institutional Investors and Corporate Governance* (1994).

'SEC Launches Investigation of Penn Central Railroad' (Abstract of article), *The New York Times*, 7 August 1972.

SEC, Exchange Act Release No. 47235. Final Rule, Disclosure Required by Sections 406 and 407 of the Sarbanes–Oxley Act of 2002 (24 January 2003).

17 C.F.R. parts 228, 229, 240, 249 (1992).

Sharpe, William F. *et al.*, *Investments* (6th edn, Prentice Hall, 1998).

Sheehan, Timothy J. 'To EVA™ or Not to EVA™: Is That the Question?', *Journal of Applied Corporate Finance* (Summer 1994).

Shivdasani, Anil. 'Board Composition, Ownership Structure, and Hostile Takeovers', *Journal of Accounting and Economics*, 16 (1993).

Shivdasani, Anil and David Yermack. 'CEO Involvement in the Selection of New Board Members: An Empirical Analysis', *Journal of Finance*, 54 (1999).

Simison, Robert L. 'GM Board Adopts Formal Guidelines on Stronger Control Over Management', *Wall Street Journal*, 28 March 1994.

Sloan, Allan. 'Accounting Reforms Won't Add Up Unless Stock Options Are Addressed', *Washington Post*, 14 May 2002.

*Smith* v. *Van Gorkom*, 488 A.2d 858, 872–73 (Del. 1985).

Smith, Adam. *An Inquiry into the Nature and Causes of the Wealth of Nations* (1776).

Solow, Robert M. 'How Did Economics Get That Way and What Way Did It Get?', *Journal of American Academy of Arts and Sciences* (Winter 1997).

Song, Jae H. 'Diversifying Acquisition and Financial Relationships: Testing 1974–1976 Behavior', *Strategic Management Journal*, 4(2) (April–June 1983).

*Standard and Poor's Bond Guide 3*, edited by Frank L. Vaglio (Standard & Poor's, 1996).

'Stern Stewart EVA™ Roundtable', *Journal of Applied Corporate Finance* (Summer 1994).

Stewart, G. Bennett, III. 'EVA™: Fact and Fantasy', *Journal of Applied Corporate Finance* (Summer 1994).

Stone, Christopher D. 'Public Directors Merit a Try', *Harvard Business Review* (March–April 1976).

Strine, Leo E., Jr. 'Derivative Impact? Some Early Reflections on the Corporation Law Implications of the Enron Debacle', *Business Lawyer*, 57 (2002).

Sundaramurthy, Chamu, Paula Rechner and Weiren Wang. 'Governance Antecedents of Board Entrenchment: The Case of Classified Board Provisions', *Journal of Management*, 22 (1996).

*Telxon Corp.* v. *Meyerson*, 802 A.2d 257 (Del. 7 June 2002).

'Thinking More About Institutions', *Institutional Investor* (November 1990).

Thomas, Rawley. *Economic Value Added (EVA) Versus Cash Value Added (CVA): Stern Stewart Versus BCG/HOLT: Empirical Comparisons*, The Boston Consulting Group, 22 May 1993. On file with the authors.

Thornburgh. Dick. *First Interim Report of Dick Thornburgh, Bankruptcy Court Examiner. In re WorldCom Incorporated et al. debtors*, Case no. 02-15533(AJG). 4 November 2002.

TIAA-CREF. *TIAA-CREF Policy Statement on Corporate Governance* (October 1997). Subsequently revised March 2000.

Toronto Stock Exchange (TSE) Committee on Corporate Governance in Canada. *'Where Were The Directors?' Guidelines for Improved Corporate Governance in Canada. (Dey Report).* (December 1994).

'Two Wall Street Journal Reporters Win Pulitzer for Coverage of GM's Turmoil', *Wall Street Journal*, 14 April 1993.

US Congressional Report. *The Role of the Board of Directors in Enron's Collapse.* Permanent Sub-committee on Investigations, Committee on Governmental Offering, US Senate, 8 July 2002.

*Unocal Corp.* v. *Mesa Petroleum Co.*, 493 A.2d 946, 953–55 (Del. 1985).

'Valuing Companies: A Star to Sail By?', *The Economist*, 2 August 1997.

*Van Gorkom*, 488 A.2d at 874.

Veasey, E. Norman. 'Reflections on Key Issues of the Professional Responsibilities of Corporate Lawyers in the Twenty-First Century', Washington University School of Law. 28 October 2002.

—— 'Delaware Corporation Law Ethics and Federalism', *The Metropolitan Corporate Counsel* (November 2002).

—— 'Musings on the Dynamics of Corporate Governance Issues, Director Liability Concerns, Corporate Control Transactions, Ethics and Federalism', 8 Feb. 2003.

—— 'State–Federal Tension in Corporate Governance and the Professional Responsibilities of Advisors', 20 Feb. 2003.

Vlahakis, Patricia A. *et al. Corporate Governance Reform* (September/October 2002).

Wahal, Sunil. 'Pension Fund Activism and Firm Performance', *Journal of Financial Quantative Analysis*, 31 (1996).

Wahal, Sunil, Kenneth W. Wiles and Marc Zenner. 'Who Opts Out of State Anti-takover Protection? The Case of Pennsylvania's SB 1310', *Financial Management*, 24(3) (Autumn 1995).

Walbert, Laura. 'The 1994 Stern Stewart Performance 1000', *Journal of Applied Corporate Finance* (Winter 1995).

Warner, Jerold B., Ross L. Watts and Karen H. Wruck. 'Stock Prices and Top Management Changes', *Journal of Financial Economics*, 20 (1988).

Weisbach, Michael S. 'Outside Directors and CEO Turnover', *Journal of Financial Economics*, 20 (1988).

Weston, J. Fred and Surenda K. Mansinghka. 'Test of the Efficiency Performance of Conglomerate Firms', *Journal of Finance* (September 1971).

'What you Can and Cannot Do if you Run a Business', *U.S. News and World Report*, 28 March 1977.

'What's Wrong with Executive Compensation? A Roundtable Moderated by Charles Elson', *Harvard Business Review* (January 2003).

Wirthlin Worldwide and Russell Reynolds Associates. *Setting New Standards For Corporate Governance: 1997 U.S. Survey of Institutional Investors* (1997). See also Russell Reynolds Associates and Wirthlin Worldwide.

Working Group on Corporate Governance, The. 'A New Compact for Owners and Directors', *Harvard Business Review* (July–August 1991).

Wu, Yilin. 'Honey, CalPERS Shrunk the Board', Working Paper, University of Chicago (2000). Available via http://papers.ssrn.com.

Yermack, David. 'Higher Market Valuation of Companies with a Small Board of Directors', *Journal of Financial Economics*, 40 (1996).

# Index

Active Board of Directors
change of company
management, 25–7;
IBM, 26; Westinghouse,
26 *see also* American
Express; General Motors;
Institutional Investor
Activism
governance and performance,
43–65; change in
governance results
in better performance,
63–5; effectiveness of
boards, 32–42; effect of
board independence, 43–7;
incentive structures/board
decisions, 74; incentive
systems for management,
75 (*see also* Economic
Value Added)
*see also* Independent Board
Agrawal, Anup, 33
Allen, William T., former
Chancellor of the
Delaware Chancery
Court, 16, 20n
Alliance Capital Management, 26
*see also* Institutional Investor
Activism
American Express Corporation,
2, 26
change of management of, 26
*see also* Institutional Activism
American Law Institute,
*Principles of Corporate
Governance: Analysis and
Recommendations*, 11n, 12n
*Aronson* v. *Lewis*, 473 A.2d 805
(Del. 1984), 108n, 109n
Ashland Oil, Incorporated, 21n

Bacidore, Jeffrey M., 50n, 52n
Bagley, Constance E., 46n

Baliga, B. Ram, 35
Barclay, Michael J., 19n
Barnhart, Scott W., 35
Barton, Nancy E., 20n
Baysinger, Barry D., 39n
Belair, Felix, Jr., 21n
*Benerofe* v. *Cha*, 1996 WL 535405,
at *7 (Del. Ch. 12 Sept. 1996),
subsequent proceedings,
1998 WL 83081 (Del. Ch. 20
Feb. 1998), 109n
Berle, Adolf, 12
Bhagat, Sanjai, 34n, 38n, 73n, 74n
Black, Bernard, 36, 37, 38n, 73n
Block, Dennis J., 20n
Bowsher, Charles A., 20n
Boyd, Brian K., 72n
*Brehm* v. *Eisner*, 746 A.2d 244
(Del. 2000), 107n, 108n
Brickley, James A., 35, 38n, 39n
Broken Engine Argument, 7–9
Brudney, Victor, 39n
Business Judgment Rule, 5, 110
Butler, Henry N., 39n
Byrd, John W., 38n, 39n, 40n

Cadbury, Sir Adrian, 116, 117n
California Public Employees
Retirement System
(CalPERS) 2, 22, 36, 44–7,
57–65, 67–8, 88–9, 94
average differential spread by
CalPERS grade groups, 130–1
average EVA™ by CalPERS
grade groups, weighted by
companies' assets, 130
company responses to request
for board governance
self-evaluation, 18n
grades assigned by, 58–62
*see also* Technical Issues in
the Analysis of EVA™ for
CalPERS-rated Companies